ADVANCE PRAISE

"Kim's commitment and passion for advocacy is inspiring. Kim's story is straight from the heart and is told from the eyes of not only a cancer patient who is dedicated to fight the disease but also a mom who is even more dedicated to fight the disease for her family."

ALAN AUERBACH, CEO, PUMA BIOTECHNOLOGY

"The journey though cancer is a complex one, both physically and psychologically. It's one I've seen many times in my personal and professional life. In STRONG[ER+], Kimberly Irvine offers a new approach—one full of determination and hope. I met Kimberly when she consulted for me; I was inspired not only by what she brought to my business and to the oncology space in general, but more so by the will and strength she leaned on to overcome her own health challenges. In her book, Kimberly shares her inspirational story of cancer and beyond, offering a change in perspective that we call can benefit from. And the fact that half the proceeds from this book go to benefit cancer research—even better."

RICCARDO BRAGLIA, HEALTHCARE ENTREPRENEUR

"There's power in knowledge. Through STRONG[ER+], Kim Irvine generously shares her story in an informative and honest way, so that others can fight cancer with determination, courage, and the knowledge gained from her experiences."

"There are no better patient advocates than patients themselves. They bring great passion, dedication, and understanding to their work—and Kimberly is a shining example of that in action. Her ability to pull from her harrowing experiences as a cancer patient and survivor while extending her hand to others by sharing her story is nothing short of amazing. Her passion and purpose comes through in her book, in her work, and I'm quite certain it comes through in everyone she comes in contact with."

"Kimberly inspires all of us (women and men) to face life's adversities with our inner power. We may not think we have it, but after reading her book, we know we can take on anything life throws at us."

"Kim is a beautiful person, both inside and out. Through adversity and challenges, she has become STRONG[ER+] in so many ways. Our gift in knowing her is that we are able to receive the gift of her wisdom and grace."

"STRONG[ER+] is an honest and moving memoir. Kimberly Irvine's compelling journey of surviving breast cancer is a story of vulnerability, courage, and tenacity. She demonstrates what it means to truly thrive, regardless of the challenges we face."

"Powerful and inspirational...Kimberly's journey shows the depth and passion of the human spirit and her determination to find the inner strength to overcome adversity...again and again and again."

"Kim's passion for and commitment to improving the lives of breast cancer patients is what makes her such a great advocate. She has persevered during her most trying moments, raising two wonderful children and teaching us all the importance of giving back while embracing every patient's journey as a gift."

"Kim is one of those patients you never forget caring for. She is an inspiration to all who are blessed to meet her. I will never forget the way she taught her children to give back or the day they brought 50 fleece blankets to the cancer center for other patients to take home. Her energy and commitment to making the lives of breast cancer patient better is awe inspiring."

KIM ROHAN, NURSE PRACTITIONER

"Kimberly's experience as a parent, care partner, patient, advocate, and oncology professional gives us a powerful, multifaceted look into the world of cancer. Her honest, compelling story is one of faith, gut instinct, and the psychological strength it takes to trust yourself and speak out. In doing this for herself, she has empowered others to do the same, beginning with her own young children. Read this book and find your path. It may not be the same as Kimberly's, but you'll be able to face it with her trusted, sage advice along the way—and, more importantly, the knowledge that you're not alone."

CHRISTINE BENJAMIN, LMSW; BREAST CANCER
PROGRAM DIRECTOR, SHARE CANCER SUPPORT

"*Kimberly's book STRONG[ER+] inspires others to become more involved in their healthcare and/or cancer journey. Her sincere story of sheer determination and strength is incredible. As another patient advocate who was quite young with two young kids when first diagnosed with breast cancer, I wish that I'd had this book to help me while dealing with my own trials and tribulations!*"

IVIS FEBUS-SAMPAYO, SENIOR DIRECTOR
OF PROGRAMS, SHARE

"*Kim has demonstrated strength and beauty throughout her journey and her struggle. Passion and resilience permeate every page of this book. She continues to inspire others to always be their own best health advocate.*"

JENNIFER MERSCHDORF, CEO OF THE
YOUNG SURVIVAL COALITION, DIAGNOSED
WITH BREAST CANCER AT AGE 36

STRONG[ER+]

STRONG[ER+]

*Becoming My Own Best Advocate
and Discovering My Purpose*

KIMBERLY IRVINE

KGI
PRESS

STRONG[ER+]

Becoming My Own Best Advocate and Discovering My Purpose

ISBN   978-1-5445-0158-1 *Hardcover*

   978-1-5445-0157-4 *Paperback*

   978-1-5445-0156-7 *Ebook*

To my two greatest blessings in life, Kalli and Tyler. May you always find strength, hope, courage, and resilience, and use your faith as your guiding light in life.

CONTENTS

FOREWORD

BY KALLI BOGARD, KIMBERLY'S
DAUGHTER, SEVENTEEN YEARS OLD

From a young age, I struggled with many things. Not only did my parents get divorced, but my mom also suffered from having breast cancer twice. I was only six years old when my mom received her first diagnosis. I was ten the second time. Throughout both of my mom's cancer journeys, I experienced several emotions. I constantly felt helplessness, fear, anxiety, and sadness. I felt as though my world was falling apart. Seeing my mom so weak and sick was terrible. Knowing there was nothing I could do, aside from be there for her, made me feel worse. I wanted to take it all away. I wanted to make everything better. I knew that wasn't possible. I realized everything was out of our control.

What we could do, though, was have faith and hope. It was the most important thing we could do as a family. Together, we began to understand what "overcoming adversity" really meant, and we discovered through experience that we should apply that to our journey. In doing so, we were all able to recognize that we couldn't let her cancer define us.

Although Mom's cancer was impacting all of our lives significantly, we needed to look past the negatives and think on the more positive side. To do that, we moved through our lives hoping for the best and living each of our days like it were our last, cherishing memories. It not only helped our family create a stronger bond, but it also made us all realize that we had so much to be thankful for. We found out that anything is possible if we had hope and faith.

Although Mom's moods weren't always the best, we all knew she was trying even when everything was out of her control. I remember during her first cancer diagnosis, I still wanted her to tuck me in every night and to come to my school events. I was young, and I struggled to understand the situation. It was hard to come to terms with the fact that my mom was sometimes just too weak to do some things. As much as it saddened me, I never realized how much harder it had to be for her—not being able to do the things for me she used to do, having to wear a wig that was most definitely not comfortable.

During Mom's second diagnosis, every day as I'd wake up and go to school, I had the same thought: *Is Mommy going to be there when I get home from school?*

Despite my constant worries, I had to block out many of my thoughts because I needed to be there for my mom, not make her more anxious. I had to learn that it was normal to be fearful, but I didn't allow it to consume me. I needed to be strong not only for myself but for my mom as well.

Every day and night, I prayed for my mother to live another day and for her to become healthy. Those difficult experiences left me quite thankful each day, though, and I remembered to thank God for blessing me with another day with my mother. As difficult as it was seeing her deal with such harsh cancer treatments, I had to stay very tough mentally.

Despite all of the negatives, I strived for growth and positivity. I knew I needed to focus on my own well-being too. Together, we all made the most of what we had. We thanked God for every blessing. Still today, we realize we are blessed beyond measure, and there's so much positivity in our overcoming that adversity together.

I am now a teenager, and I worry that I might get cancer myself. Once, when I was getting dressed, I felt some achiness in my breast. I felt a lump, and I ran crying to Mom, fearing that I had breast cancer. It wasn't. Still, of course, she took me to the doctor, and we all discussed ways in which I could **be my own best advocate** and reduce my personal risk of getting cancer. It has given me a sense of control: I eat healthy every day, exercise, and do monthly breast exams. That fear is real for me. But, like my mom, I do not want to let cancer define me. I will do all that I can to advocate for myself as a young woman into adulthood.

I will never forget a moment I shared with my mom when she had completed her treatment after her second diagnosis. We were out shopping for bathing suits for our upcoming family vacation. Mom and I were in the dressing room, and she became so frustrated at the fit of the swimsuit top. She started crying, and I felt terrible. I remember asking her if she was mad that she did not have any breasts. She paused.

"Honey, of course I get sad and frustrated, and I allow myself the time to feel those feelings," she said. "But the truth is there are so many other people who have it worse than I do. People who do not have the ability to walk, talk, hear, or see. My breasts, they do not define me." My mom was right; no one knew she did not have breasts. She was just as beautiful without them, and I saw her as a strong, confident woman. As a young teenager, that was a pretty monumental moment I will never forget.

My mom continues to inspire me each and every day. She is strong, courageous, and vulnerable to share her story to empower other women. I feel that same desire as well. I want my story as a young child affected by cancer to give other children hope. Cancer has affected my life in a very profound way, but I am so grateful that my mom is alive and healthy and soon will be sending me off to college. It's a day she never thought she would see.

INTRODUCTION

The months of chemotherapy were some of the most difficult times during my journey with cancer that I can recall. It ravages the body, killing both the bad cells and the good cells. I was sick all the time, nauseous and weak. I spent most of my time on the couch because I simply didn't have the strength to make it up the stairs.

I'll never forget this profound lesson that came during one of my weakest moments as a mom: I was lying in the living room, so sick and frail from the chemotherapy treatment. Kalli, then six, came up to me and asked if I would tuck her into bed.

"Honey," I said, "I'm sorry, but I'm just so sick and tired. I don't think I can do it."

In her sassy way, Kalli put her hands on her hips and fixed her pretty blue eyes on mine.

"Mommy, you're always sick and tired," she said. "And you never tuck me into bed anymore."

I sat in silence for a moment. *She is absolutely right*, I thought. I saw myself through Kalli's eyes: I was frail, had lost a ton of weight, didn't have any hair, and wasn't able to spend time playing with her like I used to. All I could think about was how exhausted I was. In that moment, I kept recounting in my head how I wasn't really taking care of her through my treatment. She'd been bouncing around from playdate to playdate, as I was lost in fighting cancer. In her own way, that's what Kalli was telling me—that she needed me. That she missed me.

I have to find the strength to get up these damn stairs, I thought.

"Go on upstairs, sweetheart," I told her, determined. "Mommy is going to come tuck you into bed."

She turned around and jogged up to her room, her footsteps happy.

I turned to my then-husband Mike, and I grabbed his arm.

"You're going to have to do all you can do to get me up those stairs," I told him. And I meant it.

We followed Kalli, slowly and painfully. I had to pause and catch my breath at the top of the stairs. As I leaned against the wall, still sick and tired, I looked into Kalli's room.

I'll never forget what I saw: there was my beautiful daughter kneeling at her bedside—hands folded, head bent. I could hear her sweet little voice praying.

"Dear God," she said, "please give Mommy the strength to fight breast cancer."

At that moment, I also fell to my knees, right there in the hallway. I never thought I'd hear my six-year-old daughter say those words. Tears rolled down my face as I, too, asked God for the strength to beat cancer and the opportunity to watch Kalli and my son, Tyler, grow up.

It definitely wasn't the first time I talked to God, and it certainly wouldn't be the last. In fact, my faith and my strong support system—both of which we'll discuss in depth later—guided me through not one, but two cancer diagnoses. Through it all, I never let cancer define me. Along my journey, I became *my own best advocate*, and I discovered my purpose. In sharing my story, I hope you see how you can *be your own best advocate* too.

YOU ARE NOT ALONE

If you're reading this book, I'm sure you're dealing with some type of adversity in your life. It could be a health situation, a personal relationship issue, a financial struggle—whatever is affecting you, I'm here to tell you that there is life on the other side. We owe it to ourselves to dig deep within to find the courage, hope, and resiliency to fight and to advocate for ourselves. Why? Ultimately, we have no other option. If we don't do it for ourselves, then who will?

Becoming your own best advocate means having love and respect for yourself. It comes from looking within. Remember, you have to put on your own oxygen mask before you can help others. When it comes down to it, you're in charge of the decisions you make—and you have to make the decision to stand up for yourself, especially when times are tough. In my case, they were tough—trust me. I had, and still have, moments of weakness. At the end of the day, though, I am not merely surviving in this life. I am thriving. And you can too.

In the following pages, I'll tell you my story—not just the story of having cancer twice, but also of going through a difficult divorce, becoming a single parent, losing my breasts, dating after cancer, and finding my passion and purpose in giving back to others as a patient advocate. Giving back is so important to me. In fact, **50 percent of**

the proceeds from this book will be donated to the Conquer Cancer Foundation of the American Society of Clinical Oncology (ASCO), an organization that raises funds to support research for every type of cancer.

I want to be absolutely clear: what I'm not doing is offering a fix for whatever you're facing. I can't take away your fear or anxiety. I can't remove your struggle. I can't tell you my way is the only way through adversity, and I don't have a cure.

What I *do* have is a story. In fact, we all have a story. In sharing mine, I hope you will find the inspiration and empowerment you need to move forward. At the end of the day, this is not just another book about cancer. This is a book about life, and I'm here to tell you that you are not alone.

I made it up the stairs for my daughter that day. You can make it up your stairs too, but it's going to be a journey.

Let me start at the beginning of mine.

Chapter One

———

DIAGNOSIS

"Well, you could be pregnant," my mom said. As I sat across from her at her kitchen table, I laughed.

Yeah, right. That was not possible.

I'd just told her I'd felt some achiness in my left breast. Prior to that, I was experiencing a lot of migraines, I'd lost weight, and I felt tired. I attributed it all to one thing: the stress of everything going on as I watched my mom battle brain cancer. I was supporting her as she went through her own treatment, so my "symptoms" didn't feel big in comparison.

But there was that ache. And I was not pregnant. We continued to chat as Kalli and Tyler played in the other room.

"Have you given yourself a breast exam?" she asked.

"Mom, are you kidding me?" I said. "I'm only thirty-one years old. Why would I give myself a breast exam?"

But I did. I walked upstairs and into the bathroom. I distinctly remember lifting up my left arm, feeling around my breast, and finding the lump under my left armpit. It was only about the size of a pea, but it was definitely there. I recall palpitating it with my two fingers, trying to see if it would move or not. I wasn't sure what to do, so I went back downstairs and asked my mom to take a look at it.

"I agree. I feel something," she said. "Call your doctor."

"YOU HAVE BREAST CANCER"

My OB-GYN agreed she felt a lump, but she wasn't as supportive as I'd hoped she'd be.

"It's probably a fibroadenoma," she said dismissively. "Women your age get them all the time."

For a moment, I thought she was probably right. After all, I was still processing my mother's cancer. I thought, *Am I overreacting? I am so young. What are the chances I actually would get cancer? Am I making a big deal out of nothing?*

Still, I had a feeling in my gut: Did I really know it *wasn't* cancer? It was the first of many times over the course of my journey that I would **be my own best advocate.**

"Is there any way you can go ahead and order a mammogram?" I asked the doctor. "I really want to know."

She looked at me flippantly.

"I'm going to order you a mammogram, but you're going to see that it's just a fibroadenoma," she huffed. "Women your age get them all the time."

I felt very low in that moment. Her condescending tone made me feel like I was not only wrong, but stupid and maybe a bit of a hypochondriac. I almost didn't want to proceed with the mammogram, but part of my gut was still telling me to have it evaluated. The following week, I went in for my mammogram, which turned into an immediate ultrasound. The radiologist could see that this lump was in fact "suspicious." I'll never forget the radiologist walking in and telling me the lump was eight millimeters, the size of a pea, and suspicious. He recommended a biopsy, which I scheduled for one week later. I knew I'd need anesthesia, that there'd be an incision, and that I would have to wait another twenty-four to forty-eight hours after the fact for the results.

Those days of waiting felt like a lifetime. We knew the

nodule was suspicious, but we needed confirmation from the pathologist. I couldn't sleep. I kept thinking of my children—what would I tell them? I also thought a lot about my mom—can you imagine how this would feel from a parent's perspective, especially from one battling cancer herself?

On May 31, 2008, my surgeon called and delivered those dreaded words: "You have breast cancer." I felt like I went into a fog. I felt: Shock. Disbelief. Denial. Overwhelmed. Anxious. Fearful.

I wasn't with my husband at the time, so I picked up the phone and called him. I remember he was driving, and his reaction was similar to mine: *Really? Is this really happening?*

"Did you tell the kids?" he asked.

"No, I don't even know how to explain it to them," I said. "I'm still processing it myself."

We agreed we wouldn't tell them until we'd educated ourselves about the best way to handle that conversation.

All I knew was that my kids were six and four. My mind raced: *Will I be alive to watch them grow? Will I even be able to take care of them like a mom as I go through treat-*

ment? What will my limitations be, and how will the kids be affected? How will I tell my kids that Grandma has cancer and now Mommy has it too?

The news came over the Memorial Day holiday, so I had a long weekend to process my diagnosis. I took it upon myself to research and find out what I was up against and what my options were. I visited BreastCancer.org, dubbed a "nonprofit organization dedicated to providing the most reliable, complete, and up-to-date information about breast cancer and breast health as well as an active and supportive online community." It's an invaluable resource, and the information I learned helped calm some of my anxiety. I realized I needed to form a healthcare team to help me fight the disease, and I dove in—an action that helped combat the lack of control I was feeling.

A couple of days after my initial diagnosis, I got a call from the gynecologist who had reluctantly ordered my mammogram.

"Oh my gosh," she said. "I am sorry to hear the news, but I am so glad I ordered that mammogram!"

I'm never going to see her again, I thought. *If anybody is grateful here, it's me because I trusted my gut and advocated for myself, no matter how insecure or unreasonable*

I was made to feel. I did what was right for me. Had I not, I wouldn't be writing this book today. I was ***my own best advocate.***

TELLING THE KIDS

Telling Kalli and Tyler that I had cancer was one of the most difficult things I'd ever done. I sought articles and books that were written both to explain how to deliver the news from the parent's perspective and to serve as a resource that could help kids understand in an age-appropriate way. I also talked to my doctor and another mom who was in the middle of her own diagnosis: "What should I say? How would I do it?"

I decided to use a book, *Mom and the Polka-Dot Boo-Boo* by Eileen Sutherland. It was an interactive way for the kids to learn I had a "boo-boo" in my breast. We read it together as a family, and I welcomed their questions.

As we sat on the couch, my voice trembled as I read it to my kids. Tears filled my eyes as I watched them try to understand, especially when the author discusses the spot in my breast. It was real, and I was still trying to process my diagnosis, hoping and praying my kids would be okay.

"Mommy, are you going to be okay?" Kalli asked.

I didn't want to give false promises. Although I desperately wanted to say yes, I didn't.

"I hope so," I told her. "I have a great team of doctors who are going to help me feel better. Mommy might lose her hair. She might look sick, but she's going to do her best. And in the end, we are going to pray really hard because God has the final say."

That was one moment of many to come that I came to a hard realization: it had never mattered what house I lived in, what car I drove, or how much money I had in the bank. My faith was my guiding light, and it would be there for my children to lean on when they faced challenging moments alongside me as we navigated cancer as a family.

BEING A CARE PARTNER, NEEDING A CARE PARTNER

Besides a competent medical team, I knew firsthand I would also need care partners from my personal life in order to make it through. I had just gone through it with my mom.

Before her diagnosis, my mom had been having severe headaches and would often describe hearing a constant humming sound in her ear. She and my father had just relocated from Chicago to Nashville—her favorite place and somewhere she'd always wanted to live. They'd just closed on a home. One day, she called me to say the humming feeling just wouldn't stop. She couldn't manage it. I encouraged her to go to the emergency room and get it checked out.

Another phone call I'll never forget came from the ER physician hours later.

"Listen, your mom's here with your dad," he said. "And your dad's in a bit of shock. We examined your mom and did an MRI. We found a golf-ball-sized mass in your mom's frontal lobe of her brain. It's my recommendation that you get her back to Chicago because she's going to need a lot of care."

In that moment, I didn't know what to do. I wondered: *How will I help manage the diagnosis? How is my father going to handle everything? Is Mom even going to survive?*

My mother had several care partners, including, of course, my father and my siblings. I took on a primary role, helping her advocate and form her healthcare team. First, though, relocating her was challenging, because it wasn't like she lived down the street. We were really relocating her from another state—a state where she thought she was going to retire and live out her life. Instead, she returned to Chicago to fight for her life. We pulled it off, sought the best care for her, and scheduled the surgery she needed to remove and assess the mass.

After that surgery, the doctors thought she had three months to live. There were a lot of prayers in that time. I remember sitting at my mom's bedside as she was recovering. I was crying, begging God to hear me because I wasn't ready to lose my mom. My kids were still young, and they were her only grandkids at the time. I wanted her to see them grow. I wanted her here.

I believe all of those prayers were answered because when her pathology report finally came back, we learned the initial diagnosis was incorrect: she didn't have a glioblastoma, which was the cancer on which they based her three-month prognosis. Instead, the results showed she had another form of brain cancer, anaplastic ependymoma. Even though it was a rare form of brain cancer, it was a better prognosis time-wise than we'd been given initially.

Through the initial diagnosis, surgery, and chemotherapy, my mother's support community was wide—and my father and I were leading the efforts. We had our family— both our literal family and our church family—and our friends too. There were neighbors and even friends of friends who wanted to do all they could to help. Still, the burden primarily fell on my father and me. To say it was challenging to watch her go through brain cancer surgery, chemotherapy, and radiation—watching, waiting, and hoping it would save her life—is an understatement.

During my mom's battle, Tim McGraw's "Live Like You Were Dying" was a popular new song on the radio. My mom had always been a fan of the country singer, and—seeing how she was trying to live out her days in Tennessee when she was diagnosed and had to move back to Chicago—I really wanted to do something special for her. There is no "Make a Wish" for adults, so I wrote a letter to the McGraw Foundation and told them about my mom. I didn't just get a response—I got free tickets and backstage passes for us. That night I saw my mom glow. It was like it revived her spirit and helped her keep fighting for survival. I remember feeling proud of my mom that night. Proud that she was able to enjoy the experience and forget for one night all she was going through. I learned that it was important to find joy in the little things; it helps to keep you going and reminds you that it is life and happiness you are fighting for.

Then, when I faced my own diagnosis, it was my turn to need help. It was also my turn to fight for survival.

I grew up very poor, and I was the oldest of four children. My parents never graduated from high school, and they never encouraged college because it wasn't something that seemed feasible. So, from the age of fourteen, I essentially supported myself. After I graduated from high school, I went right into full-time work. In short, I took the fast-forward approach: I went from being a kid to an adult very quickly. I don't and never have harbored any resentment toward my parents, because I knew they did the best job they could. And I learned a lot from the experience. I was always responsible and driven because I had to be. I focused on my career until I got married, had children, and stayed home to care for them.

In short, I'd always cared for myself and my children. Asking for help for myself was new, but necessary.

After my first diagnosis, the care-partner responsibility fell to my husband at the time and my best friend Brandy, who would remain with me through the entire process and whom I will reference often in this book. Other family members helped too, going to appointments when my husband at the time could not. They held my hand as chemo was pumped into my body. They listened to me when I was scared and losing hope. They gave me strength and courage when I needed it the most.

And there were plenty of times I needed strength and courage, trust me. Following my diagnosis, I never had a "why me?" approach. In fact, it was the opposite: I knew I was going to fight. Still, there were moments of sadness and anger that hit me. I was relatively healthy before my diagnosis. I ate what I should, exercised, and was only thirty-one years old. I wondered if I could have done more to prevent my risk. I was careful to allow myself those feelings and work through them with a therapist, so I didn't walk around with that attitude. I knew I needed to be strong for myself to get through the treatment but, even more importantly, I had two kids who needed me to be strong too.

LESSONS

My cancer diagnosis brought me to my knees, and I'd fall to them many more times throughout my journey—in weakness and in prayer. Still, I'm grateful that I learned so many lessons from that experience.

Care partners need support and respect for the role they are filling alongside the patient. Remember to take time to find joy and let your spirit thrive during your battle. It will refresh your spirit and charge your batteries for the continued fight ahead.

BE YOUR OWN BEST ADVOCATE

My grandmother had breast cancer, my aunt had colon cancer, and my mother had brain cancer. We have a strong family history of cancer on my mom's side of the family. I had breast cancer twice, first diagnosed at age thirty-one. At six years old, my best friend's daughter—and my goddaughter—went to the emergency room with stomach pain, and the doctors found a cancerous mass in her stomach. Six years old and boom: cancer. The point is clear: cancer doesn't discriminate. You are not "too young" to get cancer.

When I lost my hair and wore hats in public, people would sometimes approach me and ask about my cancer. I heard so many women—young, middle-aged, and old—who say they hadn't ever had a mammogram or given themselves a breast exam. I'd encourage them to schedule their mammogram and do monthly exams.

Although the man upstairs has the final say, you can certainly *be your own best advocate* when it comes to your health and lower your risk of cancer and other diseases by being proactive with your health decisions. Understand your family history, not just in terms of cancer, but when it comes to any chronic illness. Understand how your own risks will be best assessed, and speak proactively with doctors about what you can do. Don't be afraid to ask questions when you're at the doctor's office. Being your own best advocate means not always doing exactly what you're told to do. It means saying what's on your mind. It means going with your gut. It means being educated. You owe it to yourself.

As you become your own best advocate, you're also teaching your children to do the same. Today, my kids are seventeen and fifteen years old, and they've taken steps in that direction—whether it's eating right, remaining active, consciously reducing stress, or other strategies, they're aware of their bodies. They know it's important.

RESPECT CARE PARTNERS

I've come to learn from being a care partner myself—and needing them too—that oftentimes that role is much more trying and overwhelming than we think. The burden can feel insurmountable. In my work today in the oncology space, we have now come to realize that care partners have just as much of a voice as the patients do because they're often the ones navigating treatment alongside patients themselves. Care partners are vital to the mental, physical, and spiritual well-being of patients during the roller coaster of the cancer journey.

I always used to hear the term *caregiver*, but recently I started to see *care partner* being used. I have embraced the term because it isn't specific to a spouse. There are *so many* different forms of care partners. Maybe you're not married. Maybe you have a partner that you've had for many years. Maybe you're a sister. Maybe you're an aunt. Maybe you're a friend. Maybe you're an uncle. Maybe you're a brother. Whether you're a man or a woman caring for a man or a woman, the point is the same: care partners need support as they are the ones most often leading the healthcare decisions alongside of the patient.

WHAT'S NEXT?

My first cancer diagnosis was only the beginning of a journey that entailed surgery, treatment, monitoring, and—something that deeply affected me and still does to this day—the *fear of recurrence*. Let me explain.

Chapter Two

CANCER, ROUND ONE

My first thoughts after hearing my diagnosis weren't centered around myself and my own mortality. No. It was my kids that came to mind in my oncologist's office.

Oh my God. Will my four-year-old son and six-year-old daughter have to grow up without a mother? How am I supposed to be the present, loving mother they need if I am in and out of chemotherapy and radiation all the time? Will I still be able to take them to school? Will they still have playdates with their friends?

I knew that if I didn't attack cancer with the same ferocity it would attack me with, then I wouldn't be around to raise my children. I couldn't let that happen; I had to be proactive. One of my first proactive choices was to assemble my healthcare team. From my mother's diagnosis, I knew quite a bit about the process: for example, I knew I got to choose who my doctors were. Assembling a team wasn't something that happened *to* me—it's something I did. Note that healthcare teams vary based on the type of challenges you're facing. For example, in a case similar to mine, your treatment team may consist of YOU, a breast surgeon, medical oncologist, radiation oncologist, gynecological oncologist, fertility specialist, plastic surgeon, genetic counselor, mental health professional, nutritionist, integrative medicine doctor, and so forth. The list was (and is) an extensive one!

Still, no team could prepare me for what came next.

ASSEMBLING MY HEALTHCARE TEAM

After my breast surgeon shared my cancer diagnosis with me and suggested a mastectomy with reconstruction, she referred me to a plastic surgeon. It was up to me to educate myself on the process and what it would be like. I knew I wanted the best of the best doctors operating on me, especially relating to reconstructive surgery.

In my research, I found a National Cancer Institute (NCI) cancer center, one of the best in the country. They ran a battery of tests on me—poking me, prodding me, and taking blood.

Then they hit me with terrible news.

"The tumor board reviewed your pathology reports. They recommend that you undergo a modified radical mastectomy with immediate reconstruction."

I was going to lose my breast.

The feeling of overwhelming fear shocked my body in those initial moments, and that feeling didn't wear off for days. But once it did, I knew that I had to act. When you're faced with a life-changing cancer diagnosis (as they all are), you have to become *your own best advocate*. I had to educate myself on what breast cancer was, what the stages meant, what the likelihood was of breast loss, and what possible reconstruction options were for my situation. Some women can get diagnosed with breast cancer, go through minimal surgery, and do not have to lose their breasts.

That wasn't the case for me. I would have to undergo a mastectomy with reconstruction on my left side, where the cancer was located. Six months later, I decided to prophylactically take my right breast, for fear of cancer there, and to cosmetically match my reconstructed right breast.

Still, through my self-education, I discovered a newfound strength. An educated patient is an empowered patient.

By reading and understanding the literature, I was more equipped to surround myself with a healthcare team that would help me get through this with the least amount of damage to my emotional well-being and my body— and, more importantly, the least amount of impact on my children.

That meant that while I assembled my healthcare team I wasn't just looking for skilled doctors. I needed people with great bedside manner. I was about to lose my breast, and I needed people with empathy and compassion for my situation. I even preferred that my breast surgeon be a woman, so she understood what the impact would be on me if she took my breast.

Ultimately, it's important to understand that patients have a lot of choices to make as they are navigating the treatment decisions that are suggested to them. For me, I knew I wanted the best doctors; that meant the experts in my specific cancer type who practiced at top hospitals, preferably near my house. I made a list of what was important to me, and I used pros and cons lists when making final decisions. I also learned outside of my own medical journey that I could take an integrative approach alongside my standard treatment plan, such as integrating diet, exercise, acupuncture, and psycho-social support, just to name a few.

I still remember the moment I found my breast surgeon.

After extensive research, I discovered her profile and read about her history and beliefs about breast cancer. In a video interview on her profile, she said she became a breast surgeon because her mother had breast cancer when she was a little girl. I was absolutely sold. I have a daughter, so I knew she had once been in my Kalli's shoes—watching her mother fight breast cancer. She would understand my fight better than anyone else.

After I chose my healthcare team, they worked together to guide the treatment process. I learned very quickly that they could come to me with standard-of-care recommendations based on facts and pathology reports but, at the end of the day, it was up to me to decide whether or not to undergo treatment. I didn't have to go through a mastectomy. I didn't have to reconstruct. I didn't have to choose chemotherapy. But I did, because I wanted to live.

I felt comforted by the compassion of my healthcare team and confident in their abilities. Still, that didn't make the surgery itself—and losing a part of me—any easier.

SURGERY

The morning of my mastectomy, I took photographs of my breasts before I left for the hospital. I realized that, for thirty-one years, I'd had breasts. I wanted to be able to remember what I looked like before cancer took a part of me.

I distinctly remember having another thought too. *In the grand scheme of things, my breasts don't matter. I want my life.*

This was at the top of my mind because surgery came with more implications than losing my breast—and that in and of itself was huge. My healthcare team explained that the mastectomy and reconstruction would come first. Then, seven to ten days later, we'd receive the final pathology. That, in turn, would determine the stage and subtype of my cancer. This information would guide my next form of treatment.

I was overcome with anxiety on the drive to the hospital that morning. I always tell people that when you're first diagnosed the beginning stages of trying to put the pieces of the puzzle together are the most stressful. Nobody has all the facts. Nobody can tell you what your fate is because they don't know. There's testing—then waiting. Doctor's appointments—then waiting. The fear and lack of control creates an overwhelming feeling that is always at the front of your mind. In essence, it felt traumatic to me personally.

Going into my mastectomy with reconstruction surgery,

my head was spinning. *How bad is it? Do I need chemo? Radiation? Additional surgery?*

This pathology would determine not only what the next years of my life would look like, but if I would have them at all. *Did I catch it early enough? Will they get it all?*

I went into the operating room knowing that when I came out of it, I'd be one step closer to learning my fate. As I prepared to go under anesthesia, I was both hopeful and scared. I leaned hard on my faith in that moment. As they sat in the waiting room, my support community—my parents, my sister, and my best friend Brandy—was going through the same emotions. And I knew they were out there praying just as hard as I was.

After the nine-hour surgery, the first thing I remember is that I was afraid to look down. I knew logically what had happened: the plastic surgeon had placed a tissue expander inside my breast that would be filled with saline over time. Still, I didn't want to see my chest, and I was somewhat grateful that I had a compression bra on that didn't really allow me to see. I had no idea what to expect, and I wasn't sure if I was psychologically ready to look at the new part of me. Then, I was quickly hit with such searing, unbearable pain. I could barely lift my chest forward. That night, a friend stayed at the hospital, sleeping on a cot next to me. She helped me empty my drains and measure the bloody fluid. In the morning, she helped me wash my hair in the sink because I couldn't get my bandages wet. When it was finally time to shower, I couldn't bear to look down, and Brandy was there to help—a story I'll recall later when I discuss becoming breastless.

The physical pain, I knew, would get worse and would only be compounded by the emotional struggle that was to come next. Now, I had to wait for the results.

HORMONE RECEPTOR-POSITIVE BREAST CANCER

The days after my surgery were tense, to say the least. I had trouble sleeping and eating. I had many moments of despair and high anxiety, and I leaned on my support network to help me through. I also prayed heavily because I knew at the end of the day, I didn't have control—no control over how fast the results would come back or what they'd say. I prayed so hard that we'd caught the cancer early enough and that I'd be able to survive it. The days felt like weeks.

Then, the call came in. I'll never forget it.

The doctor read me the results of the full pathology: stage two, ERPR+ breast cancer. Out of all the subtypes to have, this diagnosis was favorable. The doctor said it was great that we caught the cancer early and that I wouldn't need radiation, but that I would still need chemotherapy.

I was relieved by the news and happy to receive a favorable prognosis. But still, I was nervous about chemotherapy. I'd seen my mom go through chemo for her brain cancer, and her journey was ingrained in my head. *Am I going to be so sick that I have my head buried in a toilet all the time? Am I going to lose my hair?*

I brought these concerns up to my doctor, and she was honest while trying to ease my anxiety.

"Yes, you're going to lose your hair," she said. "And we have a lot of great medicine that can help with nausea and vomiting, so we'll do our best to keep it under control. But remember, everybody responds to treatment differently. We'll help you get through it."

TREATMENT AND MONITORING

My doctors recommended I have a series of six chemo treatments, one every three weeks. I'd travel to the cancer center, get hooked up to an IV through my port, and sit for four to six hours while I took the cocktail of chemotherapy. All the while, I was hoping and praying I didn't have a reaction to the medicine. The more chemotherapy I took, the more fatigued I got. That's natural because the process is cumulative.

I wasn't in that room alone. I always made sure I had

somebody with me. I even signed up to use a calendar through MyLifeLine.org, a website platform that offers support for patients, friends, and family. The platform also had a component where people could sign up to take me to a treatment. It helped to have someone with me. Sometimes I'd bring books to read or headphones to listen to music. Sometimes they'd have live music or therapy dogs in the unit. Sometimes I'd sleep. Sometimes I'd chat with the person next to me. One thing was consistent, though: I was always grateful I didn't have to go alone. Not everyone had that option.

Chemotherapy deeply affected me outside of that room too. It takes a toll on the body. I was extremely nauseous and fatigued. The more treatments that build up in your body, the more difficult it is to go in and have another round. I also had to be very cautious about illnesses when my white blood cell counts were low. I tried to keep germs to a minimum, but there's only so much you can do. I was home a lot during that period because I didn't want to be out. I was always reminding my kids to wash their hands and change their clothes when they would arrive home from school.

In the end, to say chemotherapy was challenging would be an understatement, but I remained as positive as I could and I got through all six treatments. Then, once I'd completed chemo, my doctors said they'd keep a close eye on my blood work and complete any necessary testing. If I had any new symptoms, I was to report it to my doctor.

That's it? I thought. *Is this my next chapter? I have been taking chemo to kill the cancer, and now I'm done. So I go back every three months for blood work and we just wait and see if it grows back? What if it grows back?*

The fear of recurrence was, and is, part of my new normal as I continue to navigate my survivorship. I have learned to live with the fear, anxiety, and lack of control, but it can wreak havoc on you in the beginning. At first, in this post-chemo stage, I became overly sensitive about symptoms. If I got a headache, I would think, *Oh my God, is the cancer in my brain?* If I had a pain, I'd think, *Is it in my bones now?* If I felt short of breath, I'd wonder, *Has it gone to my lungs?* I learned that if a new symptom lasted longer than a week, I should report it. It was a delicate balance psychologically: how to be aware of my body but not overanalyze it.

For me, handling my fear of recurrence has meant constantly negotiating fear and loss of control while trying to live my life and be grateful for every day. Yes, it was and is scary—but it has never defined me.

ADJUSTING BACK TO NORMAL LIFE

As I finally started to get used to fewer doctor visits and slip back into a normal routine, my hair started to grow back. I started feeling a little more like myself, but with a profound sense of being grateful for what I had survived. My mom was also still alive, having survived her brain cancer journey.

I needed a way to give back and stay close to the cancer community. I used MyLifeLine.org to stay connected to friends and family and provide updates on how I was doing and what was happening with my treatment. In my lowest moments, it was those little messages of love and support that picked me up and got me through. I reached out to MyLifeLine and offered to volunteer and get involved. The more I learned about the company and the mission, the more I wanted to be involved. I decided to pull my friends together and ask them to help me put on a golf outing and auction event.

Brandy thought I was crazy because we didn't know anything about golf. However, I had faith; I knew it would be a lot of hard work, but that if we could pull off a successful event, we would be able to raise a decent amount of money to give to MyLifeLine.org. I called the event "Believe in Pink." To me, it meant, "Believe in breast cancer survivors just like me, believe that more breast cancer drugs will come to market, and finally, believe that paying it forward will help me never forget what I had been through." My amazing friends and family worked harder than I could have ever imagined. The event was incredible and very well supported. That night, we raised ten thousand dollars and donated it entirely to MyLife-Line.org.

This truly ignited a passion for me that taught me how sharing my story can do good for others. Eventually, volunteering for this organization opened up the opportunity for a paid position on staff. It felt like a dream job to be involved in the cancer space and know that the work we were doing was good for cancer patients everywhere.

This was just the beginning as this opportunity started me on a path that led me to where I am today. More about that later!

LESSONS

Surgery and chemotherapy were difficult, but I believe they saved my life. I'm grateful that I learned so many lessons from this part of my journey.

Having a deep sense of gratitude for surviving my battle with cancer, I wanted to give back to others. So many people helped to lift me up when I felt low, and I learned about many new cancer resources during this time. I had a desire that was growing inside of me, and I looked for a way to get involved in the cancer community. If giving back or getting involved also speaks to you, start with what you know. Reach out to organizations that touched your life personally. You never know what that can lead to, and helping others is one of the greatest ways to pay your gratitude forward.

ACCEPT AND EMBRACE YOUR SUPPORT COMMUNITY

During the surgery and treatment for my first battle with cancer, I had many moments of despair and anxiety. I tried—and succeeded, often—to remain positive and strong. Still, I am human. When I found myself struggling, I learned to lean on others and find support from my care partners. I'd reach out to women who had gone through what I was going through, and they'd give me advice. Sometimes, I'd read the motivational and sweet letters and cards people were sending me. So many people told me they were praying with me and were there with me, fighting. They lifted me up. Whatever you're going through in life, you too have people who will be on your team. Lean on them.

HOLD ONTO FAITH

After treatment for cancer, the fear of recurrence is a struggle for many patients. I never wanted my cancer to define me, but navigating the fear of recurrence took tremendous reliance on my faith. I prayed hard, I prayed often, and I relied on my faith to get me through. And I still do today. My faith has always been my guiding light. For you, if you don't have faith in your life (and even if you do), it's also best to work with a psychologist and healthcare team to manage fears, educate yourself on your risks, and understand what steps are necessary to reduce those fears. No matter what you believe, you can always *be your own best advocate*.

WHAT'S NEXT?

Going through treatment for cancer was one of the greatest battles of my life, but I knew I couldn't let it consume me. I advocated for myself in and out of the doctor's office, taking steps to lower my risk and be as healthy post-chemo as possible. Psychologically, eventually I found a balance of monitoring my symptoms and managing my fear of recurrence—which was always there. I did everything I could to lower the risk that the cancer could come back, but the thought that it *could* come back never left my mind.

Three and a half years after my first diagnosis, my biggest fear would come true. It came back.

Chapter Three

RECURRENCE

Three and a half years after my initial diagnosis, I was lying in bed and was jolted awake by a sharp pain in my ribs. I remember looking over at Mike and wondering if he'd accidentally kicked me in my sleep. He hadn't, of course, but that's how strong the pain was.

The next morning, I woke up and the achiness was still there. I immediately called my oncologist, who ordered a PET scan.

It happened so quickly: by the time I'd gotten home that same afternoon, she'd called to tell me that while the area near my ribs was of no concern, they found a mass in my chest wall that she was suspicious was cancer. My oncologist suggested I meet with my breast surgeon as my next step.

The following week, I met with her and they did their own workup of tests. They determined I would need to undergo surgery to remove the mass in my chest wall, and they would also need to remove my implant since I would need radiation. (It is not advised to radiate with an implant in place.) I still didn't know if I'd need additional chemotherapy until the final pathology report came back from surgery.

As I was recovering from my surgery, I spoke to a friend of mine who was a doctor at MD Anderson Cancer Center in Houston, Texas. He suggested I come to Houston for a second opinion. I told him I did not think it was necessary, as everything seemed to be handled well by my team in Chicago. But with his persistence, I decided to go.

Upon my arrival to MD Anderson, I had another series of tests; this time they revealed that the cancer had started to spread and that I would need chemotherapy. I was in shock, and I could not believe that this cancer had not shown up in my previous testing, scans, or surgery.

The other decision I was faced with was commuting back and forth for my chemotherapy between Houston and Chicago. I felt extremely blessed and grateful that I could afford the travel expenses to do so, but being away from my children, especially given their young ages, left me really wanting to be home. I asked the oncologist at MD

Anderson and my local community oncologist to collaborate so that I could do my chemotherapy locally and be with my children. I would still commute periodically to have any necessary testing or scans at MD Anderson, but I was relieved to have my support community around me during this most difficult time.

Another challenge I faced was having two conflicting opinions from my local hospital and MD Anderson. The recommendations for my treatment plan did not align. I found it very overwhelming to have to decide between the suggested treatments, especially since the healthcare teams I had in place were from two of the top NCI designated cancer centers. In the end, I decided to take the recommendation from MD Anderson, since they are ranked as the number-one hospital for cancer treatment. Yes, the challenge was my commute, but again I was grateful to have the resources to seek the best medical team and care for my diagnosis.

Regardless of where I received treatment, one of my main questions during this phase was about my kids. When I heard I had cancer again, my mind went to Kalli and Tyler, and it never left them: *What are their questions going to be? What are their fears going to be? How am I going to answer them now that they are older and have already seen me go through it once? Will I be able to survive this again like I did the first time?*

ANOTHER BATTLE

The second cancer diagnosis rocked my world in a way the first one hadn't. I felt every emotion I had the first time around—the crushing anxiety, the ever-present fear—only they were heightened. My fear of dying was much more intense; it felt more real. I had a long road staring back at me: I faced more surgeries, as well as more chemotherapy and, this time, radiation.

There were many times during my second battle with cancer that I was frustrated and sad.

After I made it through the recommended treatment, I struggled with the decision about whether or not to reconstruct my breasts after surgery. Ultimately, though, I decided not to. Any insecurity I had before became irrelevant. I was fighting so hard and was so focused on not having cancer that I didn't care about having breasts at all. What I *wanted* was my life.

Not only did I choose not to reconstruct, but I asked them to take my other implant out. It simply didn't matter to me anymore. I made the choice to be flat. It was a difficult decision, but it was absolutely the right decision for me. Cancer had taken so much from me already. I thought that if I was flat and giving myself an exam, for example, I'd be able to feel a lump if there was going to be one.

I was firm: no more surgeries. I didn't want to put my body through it. That meant no more breasts. That was okay, because I wanted my life, and my breasts did not define me.

LESSONS

Having cancer twice has changed my life, but it has not defined it. I'm grateful that I learned so many lessons from the second diagnosis.

LISTEN TO YOUR BODY

If I hadn't called my doctor after I felt the pain in my ribs—which turned out to be nothing—they wouldn't have found my recurrence of cancer. Much like when I advocated for the mammogram that caught my first cancer, I listened to my gut and my body. No matter what obstacles you're facing in life, remember to take the time to check in with yourself physically. Be proactive. Trust yourself. *Be your own best advocate.*

USE FAITH AS AN ANCHOR

I was raised Christian, and I went to church with my grandma, so I had a general foundation of faith before I reached adulthood. It wasn't until I got older and had kids, though, that the roots of my faith felt firmly planted.

Then, when I was diagnosed with breast cancer, my faith became even stronger. I turned to God. I asked him to hold onto me. I relied not only on him, but on my entire church family, and they lifted me up time and time again. I'm not saying my way is the only way; even if you're not religious, having a foundation to anchor you in trying times is so important. Whatever your belief in a higher power is, find it. If you don't have one, find one.

WHAT'S NEXT

I had many hard conversations when I was diagnosed with cancer for the second time—with my then-husband, with my doctors, with my family, and more. The hardest conversation of all? Telling my kids, who were then eight and ten years old, that Mommy was sick again. It would be one of many key moments in my journey parenting through cancer and beyond.

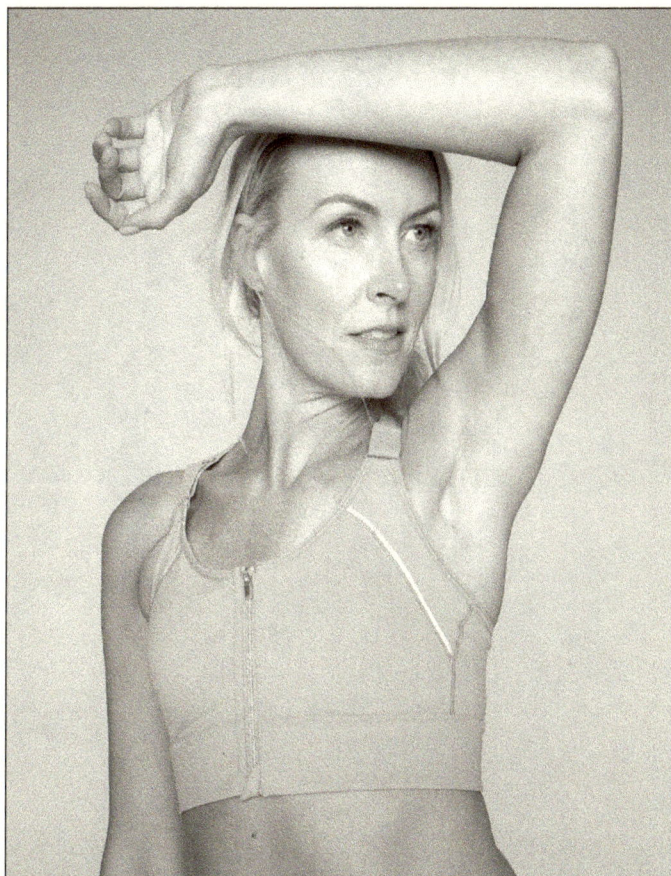

Modeling the new Athleta Empower Bra.

Example insertion of the Empower Pad.

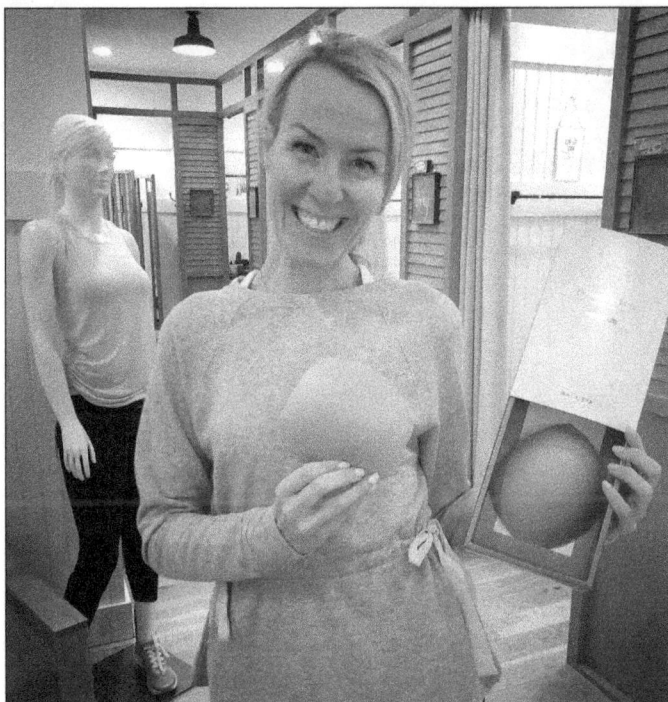

Me holding the Athleta Empower Pad.

Brandy and me at my final chemotherapy treatment.

Me and my dad.

My mom, a cancer survivor herself and a true inspiration, accompanies me to a chemotherapy treatment of my own.

Deb and I at a pediatric cancer fundraising event.

Dr. Quejada, Kim Rohan, Kalli, and Tyler after our first round of donations of blankets to the cancer center for Thoughtful Thursdays.

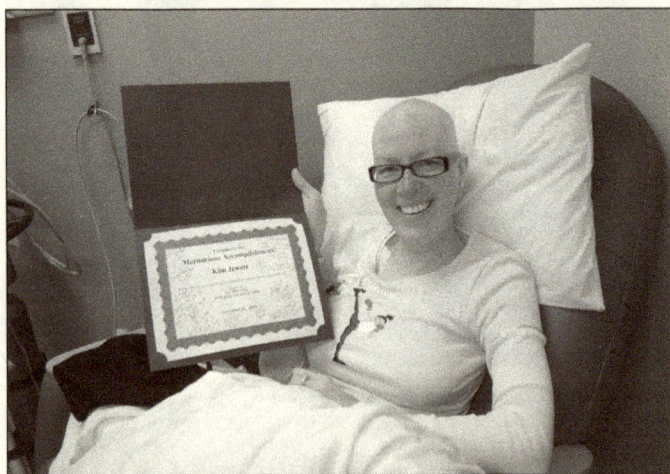

Celebrating the end of my chemotherapy treatments.

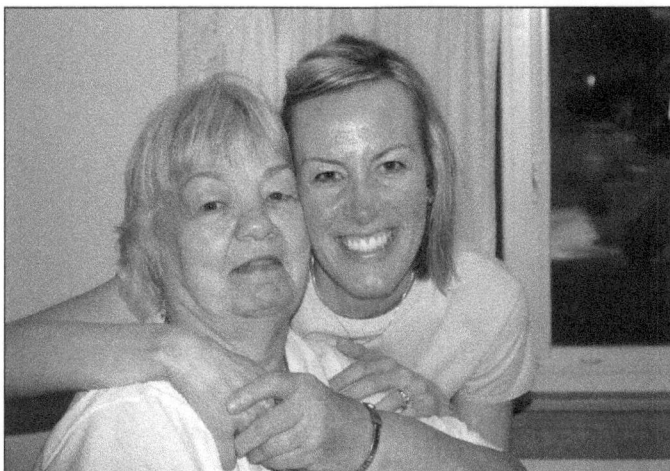

Grandma and me.

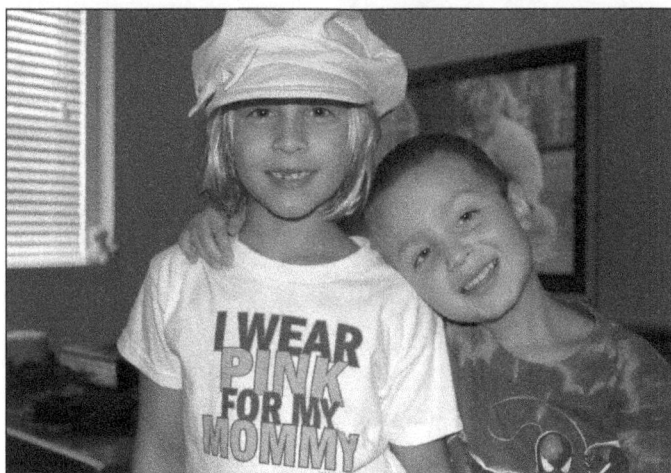

Kalli and Tyler, ages six and four, when I went through my first diagnosis.

Brandy and I celebrating my forty-second birthday.

My sister and I at a country concert in Nashville.

Jonathan and I on our first trip to Jackson Hole.

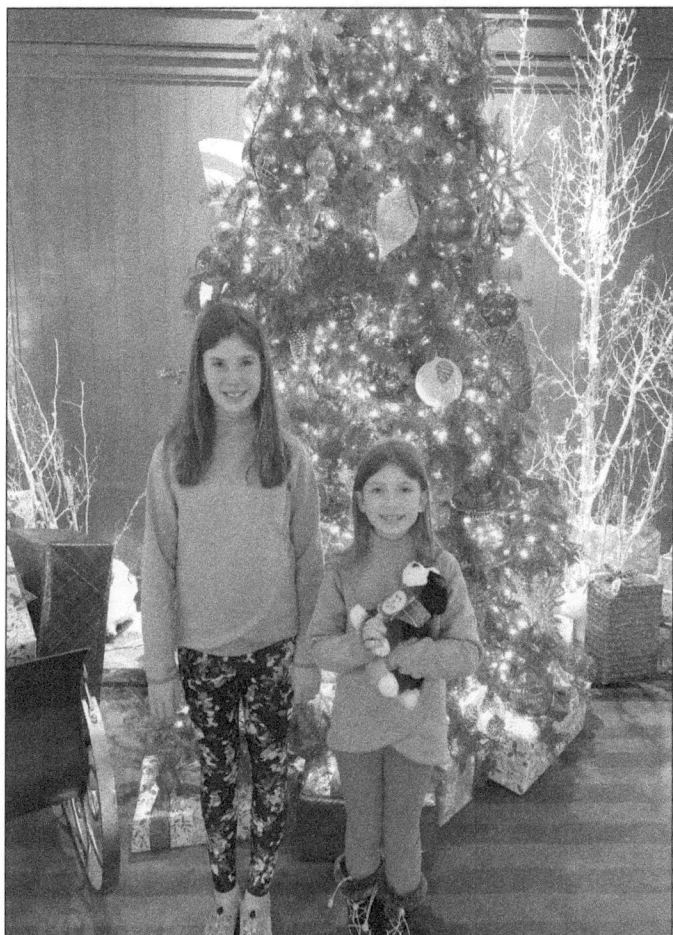

Jonathan's girls, Laura and Elizabeth.

My sister and I before I went to surgery for the first time.

Karen and I celebrating her birthday party.

Jolie, my goddaughter, and I on our way to a radiation treatment.

Jolie, my goddaughter, on her last day of chemo.

The kids and I at my fourth chemotherapy treatment.

The kids and I at our family photo shoot as I was undergoing treatment for my first cancer diagnosis.

My son, Tyler, and I at his baseball game where he wore his pink cleats to honor me and the many other breast cancer survivors.

Mary Lou and I.

Chapter Four

Chapter Four

PARENTING THROUGH CANCER AND BEYOND

"Mommy, are you going to die?" Kalli asked through tears, breaking my heart in pieces.

She was ten, so this time I didn't need a picture book to explain. She understood what Mike and I had just told her: the cancer was back. She sat next to her brother, who was also crying.

We didn't try to sugarcoat it for them. Instead, we sat them down and told them matter-of-factly that Mommy had gone to the doctor, that they found a lump, and that the lump turned out to be more cancer.

I froze, speechless. I never expected my children to have to ask me that question, although I certainly had been feeling that worry in my own heart at the time.

I didn't know the answer to Kalli's question. The only person who did was God. What I *did* know was not to jump to the reassuring answer and simply say, "Of course not," because that may not have been true.

I paused in that moment, trying to gather my own emotions and thoughts.

"Honey, I don't have that answer, but what I do know is that we have a really good healthcare team in place. They're going to do everything they can for me medically, and we're going to rely on faith and pray all the time. And Mommy is going to fight really hard."

That moment shows the hardest part, for me, of being a parent, especially a parent with cancer: I couldn't take her fear away. Meanwhile, my own fear and anxiety was escalating because it was no longer just my own. I didn't want my kids to have to feel what I was feeling, and it broke my heart that I couldn't alleviate that. As my kids' questions became deeper, I shouldered more of that burden. I was constantly thinking about my children. *Oh my God*, I thought, *I just want to be alive for these kids. They're only eight and ten. They really need their mom.*

Every damn day, I prayed.

KIDS WORRY, TOO

A cancer diagnosis isn't just for one person. It's for the family too. Along my journey, both personally and working in the oncology space, I've found the golden question when it comes to parenting through cancer is this: how do you talk to your kids about illness in an age-appropriate way?

Of course, I engaged a child psychologist to help Kalli and Tyler cope with their emotions, and I recommend that. Still, I encouraged them to ask questions and I still do today.

Over the course of our journey, I've had to check myself and have situational understanding enough to say that talking to kids in a way they can understand—without overpromising or overexplaining—is key to helping them through their journey too. I recognized their fears, and I let them feel them while delivering honest answers.

When I was first diagnosed, for example, my kids had different sets of worries: *Are we going to catch it? Is it contagious? Did I do something wrong to cause this? Because I didn't go pee pee on the potty, is that why Mommy has cancer? Why did Mommy lose her hair? Why does she look different?*

Then, as they got older, their questions became different, much like Kalli's "Are you going to die?" fear.

As young adults, they wonder: *Am I going to get cancer? Mom's cancer has already come back twice; could it come back again? She says she just has the flu; is that true? Is she lying to us?*

The bottom line is that there is no right answer. Understand that kids worry too, and meet them where they are when they ask questions. Take them seriously, because their fears and emotions *are* as serious as yours.

ENCOURAGING KIDS TO EMPOWER OTHERS

Throughout my battles with cancer, I did my best to remain positive. If I'd sat and cried, "Woe is me," that would not have been beneficial for myself or my kids. I looked at it like this: yes, we are in an unfortunate situation, and now my babies had to deal with adversity. Guess what? They're going to deal with lots of adversity in their lives, and I wanted to teach them how to approach it as positively as possible. How would I want them to handle their own adversity? I'd want them to feel their feelings but always look for the bright side. I'd want them to rely on their faith. I'd want them to know they had a loving support network around them and that they were strong enough to get through it.

As I went through my own surgeries, chemo, and radiation, I had an opportunity to model how to handle a difficult situation for Kalli and Tyler. And I took that opportunity every day. They've certainly had to grow up quickly, but I've always told them, "This is our story. Everybody has one. It's about how we write ours—that's all we have." I've encouraged them to be educated about the issues facing us as a family, and I've also empowered them to share their strengths with others. They've taken that to heart.

When Kalli grows up, she wants to work in the healthcare field. Recently, Tyler—who has always had a protective nature about his emotions and coped more internally—wrote his baseball coaches an essay on why he thought he should be able to wear pink cleats in honor of breast cancer awareness. He and Kalli want to do these things to advocate not just on my behalf, but on behalf of others who are fighting or have fought the disease.

THOUGHTFUL THURSDAYS

One of the other things I did when I was going through my chemotherapy treatments was to try to stay as consistent with our routine as I could with our day-to-day lives. Because we had just gotten out for summer break, I needed to help our nanny keep the kids busy while creating some fun! As I planned out the weekly calendar, I named each day with a theme. Monday was "Make Some-thing Monday," whether that was food, art, etc.—and so forth. Then, we also had "Water Wednesday," "Thought-ful Thursday," and "Fun Friday." "Thoughtful Thursday" was really about keeping the kids distracted during my treatment, but, most importantly, it was about how to think of others and give back. What better way than to think of someone else when you are hurting? So, we came up with ideas: participate in making meals for starving children, sit with the elderly at the local nursing home, host car washes or lemonade stands, write letters to ser-vice men and women...the list went on and on.

One day while we were sitting in the room and waiting to see my medical oncologist, we worked on the list for that week. Then, my oncologist came in to talk to my kids about what chemotherapy does to a body, killing the good and bad cells. Out of the blue, my son said, "We would like to help other people who are going through cancer like our Mommy, and we could do this on 'Thoughtful Thursday.'" My doctor said she loved the idea, and that fleece-tied blankets were a huge need; patients liked to be warm and comforted during their chemotherapy visits because the rooms were often chilly. Together, we made one blanket. The following week, I brought the blanket to the cancer clinic. I noticed a woman sitting in a wheelchair with her head down, almost asleep. I had the immediate desire to give her that blanket, and as I approached the woman (who was sitting with her husband and sister-in-law), I started to cry as I realized how frail she really was. I told her that my children had tied this blanket to provide someone with comfort and warmth, and she looked like she would enjoy it. Tears rolled down their faces as they took the blanket with so much gratitude for the kids' thoughtfulness.

A week later, I received a letter in the mail addressed to my kids. It said, "Dear Kalli and Tyler, thank you so much for your thoughtfulness. Kathy is lying right next to us as we speak, so peaceful, with the blanket on top of her, keeping her warm. In fact, the color of the blanket matches her nails too! You have no idea how much comfort this has brought her and our family. Thank you so much for your thoughtful gesture."

On the back of the card was a Post-it note that I did not read aloud at the time. It said, "PS, Kathy died tonight at 11pm."

Immediately, tears rolled down my face, and my heart was broken. Still, I felt so much gratitude knowing we truly did provide this family with comfort and warmth during Kathy's final hours.

I eventually did share this story with my kids and my community, and then "Thoughtful Thursdays" took on a whole other level. Everyone wanted to make blankets for other patients. Soon our community and even the kids' friends at school were making blankets. We distributed over a thousand blankets to kids and adults affected by cancer in our community, and I am grateful that one small act of kindness turned into a community project of giving over the next several years.

This taught my children about giving back to others in the face of our own adversity and that everyone has something they struggle with.

LESSONS

Parenting is hard enough as it is, but parenting through cancer has its own set of unique challenges. I'm grateful that I learned so many lessons along the way. And, as my kids grow up, I'm learning more every day.

EXPLAIN HONESTLY AND WITH EMPATHY

You're never prepared to talk to your children about cancer or any difficult situation. Do it with love, compassion, and empathy in an age-appropriate way. At the end of the day, that's all you have. The first time I had cancer, I used a book to help my kids understand because they were little at the time. The second time they were older, so we told them the facts and responded to questions in the best way we knew how.

EMPOWER THEM, TOO

Once, when Kalli was fifteen years old and had started to develop, I vividly remember her running out of her bedroom and into mine, screaming.

"Mommy! Mommy! I feel a lump in my breast!"

Immediately, my heart sunk. I froze. *No way*, I thought.

After we both calmed down enough, I checked what she thought was a lump.

"Honey, I think that's a piece of fatty tissue," I said. "But we should definitely get it checked out and have the doctor take a look."

It turned out to be nothing, but that wasn't the point: it was an opportunity for her to realize, as a young woman, that she had to be that much more vigilant and be her own best advocate with her health and wellness. Instead of the recommended screenings at forty, for example, hers will come earlier and more often. Both of my kids are proactive about their health in ways that leave them wise beyond their years, and that's because of the challenges we've faced together.

WHAT'S NEXT

It's hard to parent, especially as a single mother—a story I'll relay a bit later. Having cancer has given me a greater sense of gratitude for the little things. I realize I may not have had the day to be with them—to see them go to their first dance, graduate from eighth grade, cry about their first breakup. Not a day goes by that I don't think about it. Even when we face conflicts, as parents and teenagers do, there's not a day that goes by that I don't think, *This is a good problem to have. Because I'm alive to have it.*

I don't want to say that cancer made me a better parent, but it did give me more patience and appreciation for the role I've been given as Kalli and Tyler's mom. And how much of an honor it is to be here and play that role every day.

Chapter Five

———

BREASTLESS

"Don't worry. I'll come over, and we'll do it together," Brandy, my best friend of many years, said reassuringly. "You're going to be okay."

I had just come home from the surgery after my second cancer diagnosis. I had no breasts, and I knew it. I didn't want to look down. I had called Brandy that night, telling her I was afraid to see myself. I explained I was grieving the loss of my body parts. That I felt like less of a woman. That my confidence and self-esteem were profoundly impacted.

Then, she was there.

I remember the moment vividly: I had managed to take a shower, but I couldn't do much more than sit on the bench in the bathroom, still wrapped in a towel. I was so weak from recovery and so scared to see the new me.

"You're beautiful no matter what," she said. "Your breasts do not define you."

Still, I did not look down. Instead, I looked straight into Brandy's eyes, and I unzipped my compression bra right then and there.

"It's really not that bad," she said.

I knew that what had been part of me for thirty-five years was no longer there. And, as tears rolled down my face, I allowed myself to look—in that moment with Brandy by my side.

She was right. It was challenging, of course, but it wasn't that bad. I knew, in that moment, that I had to adapt to my new normal and understand that while I didn't have my breasts, I had my life.

COMING TO TERMS WITH MY NEW BODY

Although I never had "why me?" moments when it came to losing my breasts, I certainly had to adjust to my new body.

Once, Kalli and I were out shopping for bathing suits because we were getting ready for a family vacation. I tried on swimsuit after swimsuit—nothing worked. I felt unbelievably frustrated and discouraged. At one point, I sat down on the bench and started to cry.

"Mom, does it really bother you that much?" she asked, starting to tear up.

I had to pause for a moment and gather my emotions. I recognized a teachable moment as a parent: I wanted her to understand that breasts weren't everything. I also wanted her to understand that the emotions I was feeling then were raw and real—and that it was certainly okay to feel your feelings, especially as a young woman—but that I was not going to give into them.

"You're absolutely right," I said. "It is frustrating to go through this process of trying to find something that hides my scars and fits me properly. But all that really matters is that I'm alive," I told her.

I went on to explain that others in this world face challenges too—maybe they don't have arms or legs, or maybe they can't see or hear. My challenge wasn't visible to others, for the most part, because I wore a prosthesis. It was mine to deal with internally.

Kalli understood, and we had a discussion about adversity that put my situation in a different light. I explained that I will always have scars as a reminder of what cancer did to me, and it will always be hard to try on bras, bathing suits, or any kind of tops—but I can choose to let it affect me, or I can choose to cope with it as best I can and move forward. I showed Kalli in that moment, and I have continued to show her, that I choose the second option.

FROM AUGMENTATION TO FLAT

Prior to having cancer, I'd had breast augmentation. I have always been a smaller-framed woman, and having my breasts done was something I wanted at one point in my life. I was younger then—in my twenties—and implants boosted my confidence.

My relationship with my breasts obviously changed dramatically throughout my cancer journey. During my thirties, I lost and reconstructed one breast, then prophylactically took the other for fear of cancer in that breast. When my cancer recurred, I lost my left implant because of the radiation and decided to prophylactically remove the right implant because I was worried I might not be able to feel any new lumps with it there. I became breastless for good. In my twenties, I wanted boobs. In my thirties, I was fighting for my life, so I got rid of them.

Now, in my forties, one fact has become incredibly clear: it never really mattered. When you look back, some of the things you found important when you were younger were never truly *that* important. Did my boobs make me feel feminine and sexy at times? Yes, of course! Did losing them make me feel insecure and less self-confident? Yes, of course! Will shopping for bathing suits or being intimate with someone ever be the same? No, absolutely not.

And do you know what? That's okay. My relationship to my breasts has been sort of an evolution. I know now they never defined me—not having them and not losing them.

THE EMPOWER PAD

I recognize the challenge for breast cancer survivors when it comes to feeling feminine, and I'm proud to say that I've worked with Athleta, the women's apparel brand, to help find a solution. I'm a brand ambassador for the company, and I was an active contributor and tester as part of a group which the design team worked with to create a sports bra for women who have undergone a lumpectomy or mastectomy. While I worked with their product team on the development of this sports bra, I also suggested a padded insert that women could use as opposed to wearing a heavy prosthesis, which can become uncomfortable.

I knew because I'd been there: there were times I'd go completely flat. Other times, I'd wear my prosthesis. Sometimes, though—especially when I was working out—I just wanted a *little something* so I didn't look concave from the side effects I had personally suffered from my surgery. I'd take the little pads out of sports bras and put them in my bra, sometimes layering three or four at a time, but it wasn't a long-term solution.

Together, we created the Empower Pad by Athleta, and I helped them field-test the product. I also strongly advocated that they use someone who had truly been through cancer as a model instead of a fit model.

Why? Simple: as a cancer survivor, I knew what it would look like to look at that bra on a model with "normal" breasts. It wouldn't feel right.

They took my advice—and then some. They asked me to model the bra.

At that moment, my journey with my breasts felt full-circle. All those moments of despair and frustration came to a halt. My mind was racing, *You want me to be an Athleta model for your product as a flat-chested woman?* It was surreal. I knew what it meant for me, for my daughter, for Athleta, and for other women, especially women who had breast cancer.

The Empower Pad launched in 2018, and Athleta has since expanded the product line to include other sports bras that are Empower Pad-friendly. It's been an amazing process and intensely gratifying. So many women on social media have reached out to me and said the product changed their lives, helped them feel more confident, and improved their self-esteem as they went through cancer or faced recovery.

Today, I'm proud of being a breastless two-time cancer survivor, and I'm proud of the Empower Pad that helps other women who have been through what I've been through. It's just one more example of how I choose thriving, not just surviving—and giving that spirit back whenever I can.

LESSONS

Becoming breastless has not made me any less of a woman. I'm grateful that I learned so many lessons from losing my breasts.

GIVE YOURSELF GRACE: RECOVERY IS AN EVOLUTION

I experienced so many emotions after my second surgery. It was a mixture of gratitude for being alive and disappointment in feeling like less of a woman. I reached out to a psychologist who helped me navigate my feelings. They were very different feelings, but they were—and still are—both real. I'm firm when I say that just like cancer doesn't define me, neither do my breasts—or lack of breasts. Coming to that realization has been a process, though. I found ways to cope with feeling less feminine at times, and my psychologist encouraged me to channel that energy in other ways and be good to myself. For me, giving back to others is what makes me feel empowered. I also make it a priority to take care of myself and live a healthy, active lifestyle. I make time for myself and prioritize the things that make me feel pretty, such as regularly scheduling hair and nail appointments and keeping them no matter how busy life gets. I choose my clothing based on what fits me best and makes me feel pretty, instead of focusing on cost. For you, giving yourself grace may not be beauty or fashion related, but advocating for yourself and others will make you feel empowered too. Always make time for yourself and be good to yourself so you can be good for others. Remember that recovery from any sort of trauma takes time; try to give yourself the grace you need to process whatever you're feeling so you can move forward in a healthy way.

CHOOSE THE PATH RIGHT FOR YOU

I could have chosen to reconstruct again, but I didn't—and that was a choice I made intentionally. It wasn't easy. I did meet with the plastic surgeon many years after my second diagnosis to discuss reconstruction, but there was a moment when I realized I was considering that path because I was trying to please somebody else. And I was tired of it. I was completely okay with being flat.

Some breast cancer patients choose reconstruction, and some don't. Some choose to be flat, and some wear a prosthesis. None of these options are wrong. I've chosen each of them over the course of my two diagnoses, and each of them were true for me considering where I was in my life at the time.

The bottom line is, there is not one absolute way to approach the challenge in front of you. Be thoughtful, make the choice that feels true to you in the moment, and don't forget to reach out to your support system for help. I don't know what I would have done if Brandy wasn't with me for all my unveilings. Have those close to you around for your unveilings too.

WHAT'S NEXT

Becoming breastless and surviving cancer twice left me accustomed to a new normal—a new normal focused on celebrating every moment. Advice from one of my favorite physicians helped me put that into perspective. Let me share it with you.

Chapter Six

FAITH AND CHAMPAGNE

"I'll see you in three months," Dr. Valero said. It was one of my last visits with the oncologist from MD Anderson in Houston, whom I'd traveled all the way from Chicago to see. It was not typical of me to choose a male oncologist, but Dr. Valero was special: not only did he have a bit of Spanish flare, but he had a tremendous bedside manner. He was filled with passion and compassion and made me feel secure, comfortable, and confident. I trusted him. I still do.

In that moment, post-treatment, I sat across from him as we discussed follow-up appointments. My mind was a whirlwind: *Three months? What until then?*

"Dr. Valero, I'm struggling," I told him through tears.

"How do I go on with this paralyzing fear that my cancer is going to come back again? How do I deal with the anxiety? The lack of control? How do I adjust into my new normal?"

"Kimberly," he said, "what you're feeling is completely normal. Women like you fear it every day. I can give you three pieces of advice on how I would approach survivorship."

I looked at him in that little exam room, bawling my eyes out, waiting for his answer.

"Number one: have faith. I'm a medical doctor, and I do everything I can medically, but the man above has the final say," he said. "Number two: have hope. There are new drugs coming to market every single day. You never know—one of them could potentially be there for you if you need it. Number three: go home and have a glass of champagne. Live every day to the fullest."

ADVICE IN PRACTICE

The moment Dr. Valero delivered his advice was deeply profound for me, and—although that doesn't mean I don't struggle with fear of recurrence to this day—I've put that advice to work. It's helped me thrive. In fact, when people first meet me, they often comment that they love my energy or my zest for life. Facing your own mortality not once but twice has a way of changing you for the better. I know that time is not guaranteed for any of us, and I use this as fuel to truly live every day to the fullest.

HAVING FAITH

Faith has been a huge part of my process of overcoming cancer not once, but twice. As I've navigated survivorship, that has remained true. At the end of the day, I understand that doctors do everything they can medically, and I believe wholeheartedly that there is a place for medicine. On the other side of it, though, we don't have the final say. Feeling that in my heart has given me peace.

This piece of advice also reinforced the importance of showing Kalli and Tyler what it means to have faith. I have taught them how to pray, and we do it often. We also talk about how important it is to thank God and count our blessings—not just the big ones. *Every* one.

HAVING HOPE

When people get older, sometimes they grumble about birthdays. They don't want to count their age. Dr. Valero's advice has put me in a completely different mindset: not only do I celebrate the hell out of all my birthdays—which I'll explain more in a moment—but I look at them with hope. I just turned forty-two. Can I get to fifty? Fifty-five? I don't know, but I have hope.

HAVING CHAMPAGNE

I don't drink, but the "have a glass of champagne" advice is not about the actual champagne—it's about the celebration. Today, I know I'm going to celebrate every damn birthday that I have. (In fact, I usually celebrate all month long!) I'm going to live every day with as much grace and gratitude that I can and not forget any single blessing that I've been given. I'm also not going to forget the friends who are continuing to fight for their lives or the women who are no longer here. For whatever reason, my life has been spared, and I choose to celebrate every part of it.

SURVIVORSHIP AND SURVIVOR'S GUILT

I've battled breast cancer twice and come out on the other side both times. It's incredibly difficult to see those who have not been as fortunate without feeling guilty. I discussed this survivor's guilt with my psychologist many times.

"You're grateful for your life—and rightfully so. You have been spared," he told me once. "You're a compassionate person, so feeling this guilt is completely normal. It's never going to go away. It's all about how you deal with it."

I realized then that my expectation of "overcoming" my survivor's guilt was not going to be a component of my survivorship, because it was simply not possible. Instead, I learned to focus on allowing myself the sadness, feeling that deep grief associated with losing people you've come to love, and channeling it into gratitude or a way to help someone else.

Do I still have survivor's guilt? Yes. Does it hurt? Absolutely. But it also propels me into how I live my life—how I give back to others and how I parent with positivity and honesty. I try to be better every day in honor of those who didn't get that opportunity.

LESSONS

Dr. Valero's advice has impacted my life in such a profound way. I'm grateful that I learned so many lessons from my wonderful healthcare team, including him.

KEEP YOUR MIND OPEN

Dr. Valero was not just an oncologist to me; he was a friend. He approached everything we did treatment-wise with complete collaboration in mind. He not only allowed me to advocate for myself as a patient, but he helped me do it by educating me about my options and listening to my feedback.

To this day, I'm not sure Dr. Valero knows the impact he made on my life. Every once in a while, I see him at a conference, and I always make a point to hug him tightly and thank him for his three pieces of advice, which have guided my journey of survivorship.

As I assembled my care team, I'd only chosen female oncologists as a rule. Without reading any profiles, I would have never met Dr. Valero. I would have never gotten his three pieces of advice. It's fine—and good, even—to have strong preferences and advocate for what and who you want in your life, but it's also important to keep your mind and options open. You might just be surprised.

CELEBRATE EVERYTHING

No matter what your challenge is—whether it's cancer, or a chronic disease, or a non-health struggle—nobody can tell you when or if you're going to come out on the other side. We have no known timeline for being on this earth. I've learned that in a much deeper way as I've lost friends to this terrible disease. This is why I am firm on thriving and not just surviving: you can survive one more day, but it's better to make the most of it, even when you're facing adversity. It's not always easy, but it's worth it.

WHAT'S NEXT

Although I didn't have a college degree, I always felt driven and determined. I've had an entrepreneurial spirit since I was young. My twice journey through cancer helped me hone that part of me into finding my purpose: making an impact.

Chapter Seven

LIVING MY PURPOSE AND PASSION

I discovered my purpose in life as I sat in the chair, chemo IV dripping into my veins, reading Rick Warren's *The Purpose-Driven Life.*

Oh my God, I thought. *I know why I'm here.*

I'd never been one to say "why me?" when it came to my cancer diagnosis, but I could go one better: I could use that diagnosis to help others. I have never been a shy or quiet person. I recognized then that I have a mouth, I have a strong voice, and I knew I wanted to use them to leave a legacy and impact as many people as possible.

PROFESSIONAL SUCCESS

After I finished treatment and again began navigating my new normal, I decided to take my personal story, combine it with my professional skillset, and leverage it to do more good. Much like I did with the Empower Bra & Pad of Athleta, I discovered an unmet need: finding a patient-centric approach to drug development in the oncology space. Today, I consult with the goal of having patients and care partner voices be heard, and I get to improve the lives of others daily.

Getting to that point, though, wasn't so quick and easy.

After my treatment, I wanted so badly to go into pharmaceuticals and sell oncology drugs. *Who better than me?* I thought. *I've had my fair share of chemotherapy.*

Because I didn't have a college degree, though, I received denial after denial. It was unbelievably frustrating.

One day, I had a conversation with my friend Tory Burgio, who worked in the industry. That conversation would change my life.

"I'm so angry that not having a degree is such a barrier for me," I told him. "I don't want it to stop me from making the impact I know I can make."

"Kimberly, why don't you just go and consult?" he said.

I was quiet for a moment, stunned. My mind was spinning: *What? Consult? Was he kidding?*

"You have the ability. What do you have to lose?" he continued. "That's part of what being an entrepreneur is, right? Taking risks?"

I thought he was crazy, but his advice ignited a new kind of courage in me.

"You're right," I said. "What *do* I have to lose?"

At that point in my life, I'd just come out of a second cancer diagnosis. My marriage was shaky, and we were heading for divorce. I knew I needed financial independence. So, I took a shot. And it was a good one.

Fast-forward to today, and I've built a business that is beyond successful and—more importantly—helps people. More than once, I've had to overcome self-doubt when walking into rooms of male, college-educated CEOs to tell my story—only to leave them with tears in their eyes. I've testified in front of the FDA numerous times when it came to drug approvals. I've spoken at conferences, feeling internally overwhelmed and nervous, but leaving the stage with a standing ovation. Even the smaller moments—such as creating my first marketing piece and signing my first consulting contract—have felt monumental. Today, I advocate not only for patients, but also for care partners, families, and their support community. Not only that, but I've helped create the Empower Bra & Pad that helps women in a different way. I've also helped to play an instrumental role in shaping content and launching an app to help parents and children understand a new cancer diagnosis. In all areas of my life, I'm living that purpose that came to me in the chemotherapy room.

FULL CIRCLE

What I didn't know is that everything I learned over the years about cancer and all of the professional contacts I had been making was going to hit home when I needed it the most. In October 2014, Brandy called me to say she was at the doctor's office with her six-year-old daughter, Jolie. Jolie was my goddaughter, and, as I mentioned earlier, Brandy was my best friend since I was eighteen. Jolie had been complaining of back pain, and I had mentioned to Brandy that she should really get it checked out.

On the other end of the line, I heard Brandy say that they wanted to send Jolie for tests right away. They told her to go right to the hospital. Brandy knew it was serious, but I had a sinking feeling it was something even worse. She later called me from the ER and told me that they sent a pediatric oncologist to her room to talk to the family. He said that they were going to run a slew of tests; Brandy didn't understand why they sent an oncologist and figured they must do that for all of the kids who come into the ER. I told her I was on my way.

After all, as Brandy was at my side throughout both cancer journeys, I knew this was my opportunity to be by her side. Even if she didn't believe what was happening yet.

When I got to the hospital, Jolie had already had a CT scan of her abdomen because the doctors could feel a mass. Brandy was worried but refused to hear the word "cancer." She told me not to talk about it unless a doctor said those words first. My mind was racing; I was already ten steps ahead of her. I asked the nurse what the size of the mass could mean, if they could see if it was connected to anything, and when we would get to talk to a surgeon. That night, Brandy thought I was too close to cancer and projecting onto Jolie. Even though I was prepared to hear those words, she most definitely was not. We were both hoping and praying that the result would not be cancer.

The next day after the surgery, Brandy got the news: Jolie had pediatric cancer.

To be this close to a little girl who I loved like my own and know that she was about to experience everything I had gone through was devastating. I was on the phone with every contact I met from the top conferences. I already lined up second opinions and researched which doctors were leading the research for her particular cancer. At one point, I even had an ambulance on the way to transport her to another hospital, but Brandy asked me to stand down. She respected everything I was trying to do for her, but she needed to process all that was happening. I wanted to take control and advocate for her as I had done for myself, but it was a momma's job. I respected that. Brandy had been right by my side and watch me advocate for myself over and over again, and I knew she could do it for Jolie after the shock wore off.

As the first few days went on and we learned more information, Brandy often turned to me for guidance. I was always happy to give my advice and respectfully understand if, or when, they chose to go another way as a family. Brandy had to be the best advocate for Jolie because kids cannot advocate for themselves. Talk about a full-circle experience of friendship, love, and uncertainty!

Jolie fought her cancer for sixteen months. In February 2019, she will be three years cancer free. She is a little warrior. Who would have thought that beautiful little Jolie and I would be bonded forever as cancer survivors? She tells me, "I beat cancer just like you, Auntie Kim." I tell her, "You're the strongest girl I know!" and I truly mean it!

Every time Jolie has to get a new scan, Brandy and I talk about the fear of recurrence. It is the only time that I ask God, "If someone has to get cancer again, Lord, let it be me before Jolie."

LESSONS

I wake up every day and thank God for the opportunity to continue to pursue my purpose and passion. I'm grateful that I learned so many lessons along the path it took to find them.

BE DETERMINED

Not having a college degree has always frustrated me. Like cancer, it's been a roadblock. After my treatments were completed, I certainly wasn't going to go back to school at the age of thirty-five, especially as a single mother. It simply wasn't something I was interested in doing. Still, I was determined that not having a degree would not stop me from being successful. Like the cancer, it wasn't going to define me. And it hasn't.

Over the past ten years, I've built my career in patient advocacy by leveraging my passion, purpose, and life experience. It hasn't always been easy, and I've had to stand up for myself plenty of times along the way. But with determination, I've been blessed to do what I love. If you find your passion and purpose, don't let adversity or circumstance stop you from pursuing it. The journey won't always be smooth, but it will be worthwhile.

SHARE YOUR STORY TO HELP SOMEONE ELSE

Today, I share my story with other cancer survivors with the hope it can help them navigate their treatment journey. I speak on stage about what I have learned along the way. I use my experience of not having breasts to be an empowering model for others in the same situation. I'm writing this book to share that adversity is part of being human—and all our adversity looks different—but that we can still move forward if we do it together.

In short, I've faced challenges, but I'm not hiding. I've been vulnerable, but I'm not afraid to say it. I've been too weak to get off my couch and tuck my daughter into bed, but I'm not ashamed. I've gotten through those low moments with resilience and the support of others. The more you open yourself to the world and share your story to help someone else—whatever parts you're comfortable sharing—the more you'll realize you are not alone.

WHAT'S NEXT

Cancer has not been the only adversity I've gone through in my life. Not by a long shot. I did find my passion and purpose during my second cancer diagnosis, but I also lost some things too: my breasts. And later, my marriage.

Chapter Eight

DIVORCE AND THE FEAR OF DYING ALONE

My marriage had been slowly deteriorating for some time—even during my first cancer diagnosis—but I realized it was over as I underwent treatment for my second battle. I began to feel like an inconvenience and a burden to Mike; he did not have time to go with me to chemotherapy, and he did not want to discuss my disease. I felt alone and unsupported. It's important to note that I did see some of these signs before. It's hard to leave a marriage at any time, but it's especially tough when there are health issues and young kids involved.

Finally, though, I saw it clearly: we were two different people. I don't pretend to know what his experience was or what was going on in his head, because I know every-one processes difficulties differently. I respect that. How could someone who has never experienced cancer possibly understand what it's like to have it—not once, but twice? To deal with your own mortality on a daily basis? To worry about what the next test will reveal? To wonder if you'll get to see your kids grow up?

Those questions in my head made me all the more grateful for each moment—a fact he also had trouble grasping. I won't speak for him when it comes to the end of our marriage, but I will speak for myself: from my perspective, I was fighting so hard for my life. Even though men are generally less emotional than women, I still needed emotional support. I couldn't be with somebody who didn't have the level of compassion and empathy I needed and expected, through both my diagnoses and beyond. I didn't want to be in a relationship where he wasn't happy, I wasn't happy, and the kids weren't happy.

I've seen it many times: people become comfortable and complacent in marriage. They settle. They give up. Women especially can feel fearful of leaving and doubt the possibility of finding love again, especially as we age. The list of reasons to stay in a bad relationship goes on and on but, at the end of the day, it takes courage to advocate for what you want and take steps to make sure you get what you deserve.

For me, I knew that if I was going to die, I most certainly wasn't going to do it with someone who didn't love me the way I needed to be loved. So, I ended it. I knew he was never going to understand me, and that was okay. It was still devastating to lose what we'd built together, and I went through the stages of grief and loss before I finally arrived at acceptance. It was sad, but I would be okay.

When the divorce was finalized, I was officially a cancer survivor and a single mother. But I wasn't broken. I'd been through worse.

A HARD ROAD

I'd been grieving the loss of my marriage long before I actually let my husband go. After it was done, I still struggled in some moments. I did have self-doubt, wondering if I'd made the right decision. Usually, I'd quickly be reminded that I had—I have told many people divorce was worse than the cancer because of the challenges and disappointment—but it's natural to second-guess such a big life decision in transitional phases.

The hardest part of this time in my life was not that I was a single *person*—it was that I was a single *parent*. The majority of the time, all decisions and daily activities fell completely on me. I constantly wondered, *What if the cancer comes back a third time? What will I do for work? How will I financially support my kids?*

I was overwhelmed. I needed my own autonomy, as my psychologist told me, but I didn't even know who I was. Between kids and the sickness, I'd lost myself and I had to rediscover Kimberly. It was a process and a hard one to go through when you're mentally and emotionally exhausted. Some days, I would cry and think, *I can't do this. It's too hard. It's too much.*

Brandy always lifted me up in those moments.

"The only way *to* it is *through* it," she'd say. "You can't jump over it or run around it; you have to go through this. And it sucks, but you can do it."

My sister Jennifer was by my side too. She was also a support person for me, as well as a really great aunt to my kids. She is two years younger than me and single— although she has no kids of her own, my kids adore her beyond words! I always knew that if, God forbid, something ever did happen to me, she would be the next mom to my kids. That fact alone gave me tremendous comfort.

I appreciated their support, but I still felt alone at times. That's simply the reality of the situation.

Thanks, guys, I'd think. *I appreciate you and love you for being there for me, but you don't understand how damn hard this is.*

LESSONS

My divorce taught me a lot about who I am as a woman in the world today and what I deserve. Yes, there were times that I doubted myself and thought about going back. I thought about making the easy choice to try to stay together. However, having my career take off really helped me to separate those feelings of wanting to make life easy, or wanting to fight for what was best for me instead.

It was a hard time in my life, but I'm grateful that I learned so many lessons along the way.

KNOW THAT YOU'RE WORTHY OF LOVE

Although this period in my life was extremely difficult, I never once questioned that I was worthy of love. I questioned a lot of other things—why I'd stayed married so long, how I'd find someone new, what dating would look like for the new Kimberly—but I never questioned that fact. And you shouldn't either. It's true for us all. We are all worthy of love.

I'm not going to sugarcoat this: cancer, or any type of long-term illness, is tough on relationships. Suddenly your partner needs to give even more emotional and mental support, (likely) financial support, and physical support. Your day-to-day is turned upside down. If you're hurting, it can be hard to believe your partner is with you for the right reasons—i.e., because he loves you and not out of guilt or other obligations.

There were times my ex-husband would tell me he loved me without my hair, without my breasts. I almost felt as if he was just saying it. His actions and behaviors didn't always lead me to trust him, and my self-esteem was already in the toilet. The foundation was not there, and we fell apart under the weight of all the additional challenges.

I've since learned that if you cultivate a relationship that has a firm foundation in trust and emotional support—cancer or no cancer—you will be better equipped to handle what adversities life throws your way.

WHAT'S NEXT

The ending of my relationship sparked the beginning of so many new questions in my mind: *Am I going to die alone? Will anyone love me if they know I had two battles with cancer and no breasts left?*

I didn't sit with my fear long. Even in those moments of high emotion, I knew I didn't want to die alone. I knew in my heart that I deserved more. I wanted to find some-body—not just anybody, but the *right* person.

Chapter Nine

————

DATING AFTER CANCER

"Wait, you had breast cancer?"

The text came from a man I had been messaging with back and forth early into my attempts at dating using apps. I hadn't told him yet. I was never sure when to tell a new potential partner my story. After one date? Two? Three? I wanted a man to fall for me by getting to know me. Then it wouldn't matter when I told him I didn't have breasts or had battled cancer twice. On the other hand, I didn't want to feel like a fraud. I struggled to find the balance.

"How did you find out?" I asked, hands shaking.

"I googled your name," he typed back.

At first, I felt mortified and invaded, but what was I going to do? My heart sank into my chest. But I would have done the same thing too.

"I'm sorry," I told him. "I hope you don't think I was deceiving you. It's just a difficult situation in terms of when to bring it up."

That night, he was very kind over messaging, telling me he had known people with cancer before. He was supportive for the remainder of our conversation.

The next day, though, he never responded. It's how I learned the definition of "ghosting."

Brandy asked what the hell I apologized to him for, but I couldn't help it. I cried when I realized what had happened. *He had so much potential*, I thought. *If it wasn't for my cancer history...*

"You know what," Brandy told me. "That's great. You're just weeding out the assholes. If somebody is going to judge you for that, obviously you don't need to be with that person. Better they leave now than when life gets tough."

ONLINE DATING: FROM BAD TO WORSE

My experiences dating online were brief and horrible. I

tried it for a few weeks before throwing in the towel. I emotionally invested in people several times. I got caught up in the excitement and romance, and then the balloon would inevitably pop. I got knocked down several times, sometimes in not-so-nice ways.

One man asked if I was going to die—not the first time I'd been asked that question, but the first time I'd been asked by an adult over dinner. I felt slapped in the face when he asked. I knew if he couldn't handle that conversation, he definitely couldn't handle the one where I'd need to tell him I no longer had breasts. In that situation, I found a way to end the date as soon as possible.

In another situation, I dated someone for almost a year. When we decided to break up, he told me that he was not okay with the fact that my body was different. He was incredibly superficial, clearly, even though he was supportive during the year we dated. It was traumatic for me. *How can someone be so selfish?* I thought. *How did I miss this part of him?* He never showed that at all; I realized very quickly that I couldn't allow myself to be sad over dirt bags like that. I had to believe I could find someone who saw past my being breastless and saw my resilience and strength; that's who I really wanted to be with. Finding him was harder than I'd thought.

Between trying to decide when to deliver the news about

my cancer and explaining the body it left me with, my anxiety around dating was through the roof. I decided to try to meet someone organically. I never had a problem meeting people because I was magnetic and easy to talk to, as my best friend would say. I wanted my personality and energy to help me find someone, not my profile. I'd talk to people in restaurants, on airplanes, and other places when out and about. I had some friends who refused this technique, and I always told them, "It's not like someone is going to come knocking down your door. You've got to get out there." I took my own advice.

As frustrated and discouraged as I was, I still believed—and prayed—that God would allow me to find someone to spend my life with because I knew that's what I needed.

INTIMACY POST-SURGERY

After I lost my breasts, intimacy scared me. It was challenging enough to be in the bedroom with my husband when I was married, but it was another thing altogether to re-learn how to become intimate with someone new.

I always wondered what they thought when I brought up the conversation. In the back of my mind I thought, *I wonder if this man knows what I mean when I say I don't have any breasts. I wonder if he understands. Does he think I have reconstructed breasts because I'm wearing prosthetic breast inserts now? Oh God, what if we get to the point where he puts his hand up my shirt, and he feels my prosthesis? What if it pops out in the moment?*

I tried to overcome my insecurity about my body by wearing clothing, such as negligees, that made me feel more feminine. I had to allow myself that grace. It was a huge step in vulnerability; in your twenties and thirties, many of us are a little more free with ourselves and our mates in terms of how and who we connect with on a sexual level. For me, I truly had to care deeply about someone if I was going to be vulnerable enough to share that part of me. I certainly wasn't out looking for one-night stands. I wanted an intimate and real love, in and out of the bedroom.

A GREAT GAME OF CHESS

I did find love, and it came full-circle in more ways than one. I met my current partner, Jonathan, when his wife at the time, Kara, someone I knew, was fighting stage four breast cancer. I was dating another man at the time, and our families became fast friends. We went to Cubs games with our kids, and I even joined them at their anniversary dinner. Once she knew that hospice was near, I wanted to create a memory that would profoundly impact their family when they needed it the most. Since their family was huge Cubs fans and loved Ben Zobrist, one of the players on the team, I reached out to the Cubs to see about granting a wish for their family to meet him. With the help of the Cubs and a dear friend of mine, we arranged for their family to meet not only Ben Zobrist, but many other Cubs players too, during batting practice. It was a moment they will all never forget. I will never forget Kara looking at me and telling me as we were waiting for the game to start, *"Today could not be any more perfect, Kim. I am so grateful. I actually forgot I had cancer."* They had two daughters, who were seven and nine at the time.

Sadly, I learned that the clinical trial she was part of didn't work, and Kara went into hospice, so my communication with her slowed drastically. She just wasn't able to keep up. I'd check in with her husband, Jonathan, to see how she was doing.

"Hey, she made it to Christmas," I remember reading one morning as Kalli and Tyler unwrapped gifts at my feet. *Oh my God, I'm so happy for her,* I thought. *She got to see Christmas with her girls. What a blessing.*

Then, scrolling through Facebook after the New Year, I saw his gut-wrenching post. She'd died that morning. I'll never forget that moment—it was the most intense survivor's guilt I'd ever felt. Why was her life taken, but mine spared? Her kids were close to the same ages as mine were when I was going through my second diagnosis. I felt horrible for her husband, who was now a single dad. So many emotions flooded me.

I wasn't able to attend her service, because I had a business trip that conflicted, and—to be honest—I couldn't bear to do it at the time. It hit too close to home. Still, I felt deeply for their family, and I sent a sympathy card and donated to the girls' education funds.

"I just received your card," he texted me soon after. "Thanks so much. That was very generous."

"You're welcome. How are you? How are the girls?" I responded.

After that, the conversation opened. He had someone he could talk to and relate to, which was difficult for such a private person. We remained friends for quite a while, and I supported him as he handled being a newly single dad and struggled with the grief of losing his wife. I remember once, he called me for help because his seven-year-old daughter had been crying so hard in bed for her mother that she was vomiting. He didn't know what to do. My heart ached for all of them.

Eventually, both of us opened up about the fact that we had feelings for each other. We also had immense guilt: *Are we doing something wrong?* We didn't see each other often because of the distance, but we talked often and kept it quiet. We did what we could to foster a friendship that was continuing to blossom.

His late wife's birthday—she would've turned forty that July—was the midpoint in the loss for him, and he hit a wall of major grief. He wanted to take a break and go to grief counseling. I understood; he was dealing with not only his own emotions, but those of his daughters too. He said he didn't even know how to make it through the day sometimes. That he still walked into rooms on occasion and thought she would be there. It was the other side of grief I'd never seen.

I supported his decision. I was ready and wanted to move forward, but I also genuinely cared about him as a person and wanted him to process his emotions. Those questions surfaced again: *Should we keep talking? Is this even okay?*

We kept communication alive as he went through his intense grief, and I continued to support him as a friend. I wanted to pursue a relationship with him, but I knew there were still many questions. He worried about dating someone else who had cancer. Would he lose me too? I worried if he'd be ready to move on, because I didn't know how long I had to wait.

Then, in mid-October, he told me he was ready. It didn't

mean he wasn't going to have a hard time, he said, but he felt like he was finally in a place to find happiness again.

And we did find happiness together, and we've been going strong ever since. He says he believes his wife played a great game of chess in bringing us together. I agree.

There is no guarantee at what the future holds. Hopefully this love will last; maybe it will not. What I have learned throughout my journey is to enjoy every day and live in the moment. I am happy and hopeful for the future and, if nothing else, the opportunity to experience a deep love, affection, and connection to another person who understands me and celebrates who I am trying to be in this world.

LESSONS

Dating after cancer was not always fun, but one thing was certain: I knew I hadn't fought so damn hard in my life to be alone. I'm grateful that I learned so many lessons from putting myself back out there.

ADVERSITY DOESN'T MAKE YOU UNLOVABLE

Although dating was difficult (to say the least) and I sometimes doubted I would find someone, I never doubted that I was deserving of love. In fact, I believe adversity makes us able to be even more open to the right love when we find it because we've gone through so much to get there. The "going through it" that Brandy talked about as I went through my divorce *did* eventually lead to the "getting to it." I just had to wait for the timing to be right and for God to deliver. Patience was key.

SHOW YOURSELF TO THE WORLD

If you're trying to date after cancer or after any type of adversity, people aren't going to come find you on their own. I had to put myself out there. I had to be emotionally available and vulnerable in order to find a partner who was too. Show yourself to the world because there are people out there who want and need to see you as you are.

WHAT'S NEXT

My romantic life has come full-circle, and so have other areas of my life. Today, I feel more grateful and blessed than ever before. Let me tell you why.

Chapter Ten

GRATEFUL AND BLESSED BEYOND MEASURE

As of this writing, I am forty-two years old. My fortieth birthday, in particular, was a big milestone for me. Yes, it's true that my thirties were a difficult decade for more reasons than one, but they've left me grateful and blessed in many ways. Instead of walking on eggshells and feeling bitter because my experience hasn't been as I'd expected it, I've fully embraced this next decade of life.

I'M RICH IN WHAT MATTERS

I am still fearful about the cancer possibly returning, but the anxiety has dissipated over time. It will always be there to some degree. I've learned to deal with the new normal: that my cancer is in the rear-view mirror, but that I need to be vigilant about my health and be aware that it could return. Not a day goes by that I'm not thankful for my life.

As people, we can be rich in so many things in this life. I am rich in health, family, and love. The love comes from all around. I had an older friend, Mary Lou, who passed away a few years ago. As she was nearing the end of her life, we had a conversation about how difficult it is to face your own mortality. Something she said will always stick with me.

"Kimberly, you have such a great spirit, and you've helped me through this journey with cancer. Now, it's my end stage of life. I hope that someday you'll see that I'm a guardian angel for you and that you're going to find the love you so richly deserve," she said.

When she passed, she left me a hand-sewn gift and a note, telling me she would watch over me and bless me. Every time I look at it, I remember how blessed I already am. I've built a business without having a college degree. I continue to be a single parent to Kalli and Tyler every day. I get to help patients advocate for themselves and improve their experience as they face some of the hardest battles of their lives. I feel like I am finally living the purpose-driven life that God had intended for me. It was a difficult road to get here, and oftentimes I had lost hope. But I held onto it, and I am so grateful I did.

When I have moments of survivor's guilt, I realize this is all God's plan. There is no doubt in my mind that God has a plan for me. When I struggle, I simply talk to God. *Continue to use me*, I pray. *Continue to use me throughout your process and allow me to help other people.* When I do that, I heal myself. And healing is never done.

And, as I continue to fall deeper in love with my partner, I can't help but be hopeful that this is the next chapter God intended for me. We've gotten past the fear, anxiety, and guilt we once had. Instead, we know the truth: we've found love on the other side of grief. He had to move through his grief until it was manageable, and I had to overcome my feelings of wanting to run away for fear that if I died, I'd leave him and his kids once more. If anyone says we haven't tested our relationship, they're wrong; we've done so in a very powerful way.

LESSONS

There's been one theme in all the lessons from the previous chapters: ***GRATITUDE.*** Remember that somebody, somewhere has it worse than you do. Take your battle and use it in a powerful way. Connect with others, share your story, and take the time to listen. In my lowest moments,

I always knew things could get worse and was grateful for my struggles and the opportunity to overcome them. Nowhere is that more evident than in these reflections.

CHERISH THOSE WHO SUPPORT YOU

I know as well as anyone that no time is promised, and you make time in this life for who you want to make time for. There have been people in my life consistently who have made time for me, even when it was hard. I've named several in the acknowledgments of this book, and Brandy is one of those people. I'm blessed and grateful that she has always been my first call. My connection to her has been so strong that people joke about us being sisters. When I told her I wanted to start a business, she built my website in one night. She trucked to my house in the middle of the night on a moment's notice many times, if I just said the word. And now, even though I don't have a lot of free time, I'd do the same for her. Actually, I'd do the same for anyone in my emotional support network—my family, my close friends, the people who mean the most to me who were there to help me get to the other side. I'm sure if you look around you closely, you'll find those same people in your own life. Cherish them.

NEVER FORGET YOUR FAITH

When my then-six-year-old goddaughter was diagnosed

with cancer, I remember praying, *God, give me the cancer and not her. I'm an adult, and she's just a child.* Her mother is the one who changed my bandages and was there for me at every turn. I have lived through so much, and I prayed with all my might that God would spare her too. And He has.

You will face trying times. That's part of life, and some times are harder than others. But if you have faith and love those around you, you can not only survive whatever you're going through—you can thrive.

WHAT'S NEXT

The ultimate answer to my last "What's Next" piece of this book is simple: I don't know. We never do. But what I do know is that I will continue to follow God's plan. I have learned that God is always with me, so I don't have to succumb to terror and discouragement! Instead, I can focus on the strength and courage that God will give to me if I only ask:

"Have I not commanded you? Be strong and courageous. Do not be terrified; do not be discouraged, for the LORD your God will be with you wherever you go."

—JOSHUA 1:9

CONCLUSION

We all struggle with some type of adversity in our lives, whether it's a health concern or a relationship issue—the list goes on and on. Sometimes, that adversity can be hard to accept. It can be easier to cower from it. It can feel safer to put your head down and think, *I can't do this. It's too overwhelming.*

I'm here to tell you that you *can* do it. Allow yourself the confidence to lean on your support community. Find your courage and strength. If you have faith, lean on it. Allow yourself to be vulnerable. That last part is hard. I wasn't always this vulnerable, but I've gotten to a place of overcoming shame and speaking my truth. I've evolved and continue to do so, even today. I have educated myself with self-help resources like the work of Brené Brown, who has helped me better understand shame and vulnerability.

Although the adversities we face may be different, my story is no different than yours. We are all on this journey of life together. If you can advocate for yourself and trust in something greater throughout life's challenges—without letting them define you—you'll come out far stronger.

My hope in writing this book is to empower you and to help others on a bigger scale. Remember, 50 percent of the proceeds from this book go to the Conquer Cancer Foundation of the American Society of Clinical Oncology (ASCO), an organization that raises funds to support research for every type of cancer.

In the big picture, I hope my story ignites a greater purpose for you to give back, whether you do with money, time, or both. When we face challenges, it's easy to get lost on focusing inward. When we look to others and try to see what value we can bring to their lives, it helps us too.

You've read my journey, and I have shared how I use my story to inspire others. Visit my website (KimberlyIrvine.com) and share your story of feeling inspired and empowered to **become your own best advocate**! Keep moving—I'm here with you.

Kalli, Tyler, and me at the Cubs game on Mother's Day, 2018

ACKNOWLEDGMENTS

Above all, to God: my guiding light and Savior who has blessed me way beyond measure.

I am truly grateful and blessed to have the following people who have played an essential part in my life. I would not be the woman I am today without your support, guidance, and unconditional love.

FAMILY

My parents: Thank you for doing the best you knew how to, and for loving your grandkids and supporting me throughout my journey. Mom, you're stronger than you will ever know. I am here because of you.

Kalli: You are the most amazing, smart, kind, thoughtful, driven daughter a mom could ever ask for. Your compassion for others and desire to make a difference in the world, combined with your drive to succeed, is inspiring and empowering. May you always hold onto your faith as you grow into the woman you were meant to be. I am so very honored to be your mom.

Tyler: The first boy who will always have my heart. I admire your passion for baseball, your compassionate heart, and your ability to have empathy for other people. My wish for you is that you continue to chase your dreams and know that I will always love you beyond measure. My greatest blessing has been being a mom to you and your sister, and I am forever grateful for that role.

Jennifer Irvine: You are my sister and friend. I'm sorry for always stealing your clothes when we were younger. Clearly my daughter has paid me back in more ways than you will ever imagine. Thank you for always loving my kids unconditionally and making me laugh when I needed it most.

Susan Saylor: My aunt and inspiration. Thank you for showing me unconditional love with the care and love you had for your son, Keith. I continue to be inspired by you as a mom, modeling that same compassion. Your strength and courage fighting cancer has also fueled me when I went through cancer twice.

Jeff Porys: My uncle, who loved me like a daughter, and

someone I felt genuine love from as a little girl. Thank you for loving me unconditionally and supporting me through life's adversities. I am proud of the man you are today and the unconditional love you gave my grandmother before she went to heaven.

Jonathan: We found love in the heart of grief, and I believe someone played a great game of chess. I am enjoying the journey with you and the kids, wherever it leads.

FRIENDS

Brandy Kneip: You have been my very best friend for the last three decades of life. The ying to my yang. I honestly would not be who I am today without your unconditional love and support. You have always had my best interests at heart and have kicked my butt when I needed it most. Our friendship is one I will forever cherish for the rest of my life, and I am so grateful Jolie is healthy now.

Karen Korol: You are one of my best friends who gave me support and love when my kids and I needed it the most. The memories we created before cancer will always be cherished, and so will the life we are living now alongside our kids—I am grateful my daughter loves you and trusts you just as much if not more than I do!

Debbie Gallagher: You are strong, empowering, and independent. Thank you for your unwavering support and guidance. You inspire me in so many ways.

Marci Wirtz: Without you, I am not sure I would have made it through my second diagnosis. You took care of me and my kids when we needed it the most and helped support our "Thoughtful Thursday" blanket project. You inspired my kids and loved them when they needed it the most—and words will never express the immense gratitude I feel for the time you afforded our family.

Kim & Dan Kittleson: Kim, my survivor sister friend, who is always thinking of others and appreciating the greatest gift of life alongside me and embracing it with wonderful memories. Your support for me and my family over the last decade has been instrumental in my healing journey. Cheers to the next decade of healthy life together, my friends!

Michelle Rosch & Amanda Shields: My survivor sisters! Thank you for supporting me during my journey with cancer and divorce. Your own personal journeys have inspired me and given me the courage and strength I needed to get through my own. While we may not see each other as often as we would like, our friendship never fails. Cheers to our health and embracing the life we fought so hard for. And for the precious miracle babies you're watching grow!

GUARDIAN ANGELS

Grandma Frances: My guardian angel, who I miss so very much. We will always have a special bond with our breast cancer diagnoses, and I am grateful for the unconditional love you showed me as a child. You allowed me another place to call home when I needed it the most, and I am forever grateful for that support. May you rest in peace.

Mary Lou: Even though we only knew each other a very short time, I am blessed for the time we had. I know you are another angel watching over me and guiding me through life. I am forever grateful for our many conversations that have given me the confidence and self-esteem to know I am deserving of love. You will always hold a special place in my heart.

HEALTHCARE TEAM AND PROFESSIONAL MENTORS

Dr. Quejada: You're one of the most compassionate oncologists I've ever known. Thank you for saving my life and allowing me to be the woman I am today.

Dr. Valero: Your three pieces of advice continue to guide me through life, and because of you, I am alive and thriving.

Dr. Keegan: Psychologically, I am not sure where I would be today without your guidance and support. It certainly has been a journey but, because of you, I am the woman I am today: strong, courageous, confident, successful, and independent. "Thank you" is not enough for the impact you have made on my life, personally and professionally. This book is driven because of you too!

Kim Rohan: Thank you for always taking good care of me and my kids when we needed it the most. Life certainly threw me a lot of adversity, but you were always there to bring me through it and give me strength and courage when I needed it the most.

Susan Gorky: You have inspired me personally and professionally, and I am forever grateful for our friendship. May you continue to have good health and happiness as you so richly deserve.

Sarah Krug: Thanks to you, my wardrobe is on point. Life keeps us both busy, but I know who I can count on personally and professionally. Thank you for your friendship and for inspiring me with your passion and compassion for others. I admire your brain and your fashion!

Tory Burgio: Thanks to you, I had the courage to become an entrepreneur and build a brand that I never dreamed of, personally and professionally.

Sheryl Lapidus: You are a friend who supported me

throughout my fight and my professional career, while inspiring me as a single mom.

Robert Doig: Because of you, the title of my book exists and is so powerful and meaningful. I am extremely appreciative of your support—and for taking the time to wear your marketing hat, combined with your own personal survivorship passion.